ME AND MY SHADOW

Babs Wilson

Published by New Generation Publishing in 2022

Copyright © Babs Wilson 2021

First Edition

The author asserts the moral right under the Copyright, Designs and Patents Act 1988 to be identified as the author of this work.

All Rights reserved. No part of this publication may be reproduced, stored in a retrieval system or transmitted, in any form or by any means without the prior consent of the author, nor be otherwise circulated in any form of binding or cover other than that which it is published and without a similar condition being imposed on the subsequent purchaser.

ISBN
	Paperback	978-1-80369-161-9
	Hardback	978-1-80369-162-6
	Ebook	978-1-80369-163-3

www.newgeneration-publishing.com

This is about my beloved brother Brian and all the love and music he has given to me and to ALL his many friends and fans worldwide throughout his life.

I DEDICATE THIS BOOK TO ALL OF YOU.
XX

FOREWORD

From Babs Wilson (little sis!)

I feel highly honoured and happy to have the opportunity to write about my beloved brother Brian, and really hope that I can do him justice in conveying what a remarkable man he has been in his life and the tremendous love he has shown to me and the many people he has been involved with during his lifetime.

I have loved him always with all my heart and even though we have spent long times apart, because of his career and living many miles away from us in London and Wales, on the many times we got together again, it was as if we had never been away! And those wonderful bear hugs!!.... I am sure many have experienced these too and will have great memories of them xx.

It was always very sad to say our goodbyes after our get-togethers, and we always had to depart rapidly from each other, which was usually at a train station, but since he has gone away permanently from this earth, it has been absolutely dreadful but **memories** and **love** will be **forever treasured in our hearts**.

This documentation I have written into this book are from Brian's written and spoken words to me and his friends. I have titled these as **Brian's words:**, and my own personal experiences of Brian, I have titled as **Babs' words:**.

The rest of the book is filled with personal stories, experiences and tributes from many of his friends and fans.

Our Brian is and always will be
MY FOREVER SHADOW.
Enjoy and much love
Babs xx

SPECIAL THANKS

I would just like to say a huge and humungous thanks to you all for being Brian's friends and fans, and all the love you have shown to him. I know for certain that Brian always appreciated this and felt so much of your love.

I do apologise that I can't include everyone as this would be impossible unless other books were written (and in different languages, and with photo albums included)!! I really hope that one day I can get to contact and meet some of you to say a personal thank you if I have not already done so (and a hug too if I am allowed).

I thank everyone who has written and told me lovely things about Brian and to everyone who has supported me during Brian's illness and his departing of this world, and continue to support me with words, tributes, music, photographs, phone calls and messages etc. I am deeply touched and grateful.

My biggest support of course is my husband Dave who is constantly helping and encouraging me. Brian always loved him deeply too as a brother and friend, ever since they met in 1967 when Dave and I started our life together as a couple. We have had many special times together with much laughter and tears and helping each other when needed.

Brian's final days were extra special, valuable and wonderful. We shared so much in a short time, and we truly appreciated and loved each other.

Every single day we were together (and often more than once in a day) Brian would say to me "Don't forget, you are my one and only and I love you very much… and Dave, I give you a bunch of fives and look after my shoes!!" (And that's another story... !)

My biggest and most special thanks go to Brian's special close friend David Harrison, for his time spent with Brian, and his documentation of Brian's words and photos obtained.

David was a fellow musician and an excellent drummer and he and Brian played at many gigs together. They were great personal friends and had a lot in common with each other and would spend hours talking together, usually at Brian's bungalow in the conservatory whilst looking over the wonderful views of North Wales.

Brian loved to tell David his life stories and experiences and David was the ideal trusted friend to listen and document everything he said, of course with Brian's permission, as there were some "loose plans" between them that eventually these stories might be included in a book, and David also gathered many photographs of Brian and placed them into an album.

David and Brian played a gig for me on my 60th birthday celebration at Skegness, alongside many other musicians, friends and relatives, and David, Brian and I had a discussion then about the possibility of writing a book on Brian's life, and David gave me his album of photographs that he had planned to include with the book as my 60th birthday present.

Unfortunately, and very sadly, Dave fell ill and was unable to continue his conversations with Brian and had to discontinue his music and writings. He was supported and cared for by his lovely wife Carol and family until his death. Brian was very fond of them and loved them both dearly.

Thank you, Carol, for allowing me to read and use David's documentation in this book.

After Brian's death, I also found several pages of handwritten documentation written personally by Brian on various aspects of his life, and I have included these alongside David's documentations and also put them together under the heading of **Brian's words:**

Special thanks also go to Brian's dear friend Iain Purdon, fellow musician and member of the North West Shadows Club, who had stored Dave's writings after being given them by David's wife Carol, and, after a personal discussion between us all, Carol gave permission for Iain to send them to me for inclusion in my book.

Iain also very kindly sent me his own personal interview of Brian via his fantastic video tribute, words and music (on YouTube), and some brief written reminiscences of Brian's pre-Shadows days from another personal interview with Brian.

Dave Wilson and Brian

David and Carol Harrison

Iain and Jeannie Purdon

Here we go!

THE YOUNG ONE

Introduction from David Harrison 2011

From the Toronto Hilton in Canada to the Ham and Cheese at Scaggelthorpe and the Spotted Cow at Malton in Yorkshire, from the Wednesday night hop at Marco's in Grantham to the London Palladium, Brian's music has no boundaries.

These pages are the stories that are part of the life of Brian "Licorice" Locking.

Starting his musical career as a young boy playing his sister's plastic mouth organ and finding his personal fame as a bass player for the top American and UK rock 'n' roll artistes, including Conway Twitty, Eddie Cochran, Gene Vincent, Brenda Lee, Wee Willie Harris, Vince Taylor, Terry Dene, Tommy Steele and Marty Wilde, eventually taking over Jet Harris's prestigious position as bass guitarist for Cliff Richard and the Shadows.

Brian's performances with the Shadows were during their period of highest instrumental successes: "Guitar Tango", "Dance On", "Foot Tapper", "Atlantis" and of course the filming of *Summer Holiday* with Cliff.

Brian is still working at keeping the music of the Shadows alive throughout the world and is an essential part of the programme each year for Bruce Welch's *Shadowmania* event in the UK.

Brian is an international ambassador for Shadows music playing both bass guitar and his harmonicas at

Shadows clubs and concerts in the UK and around the world.

From his days as a backing musician for top artistes, Brian had definitely come "out of the Shadows" as a bass player in the background to take centre stage as a solo performer in his own right.

As Brian used to sit and recall his memories to me at his home in North Wales, I suggested that these memories should be made available in book form, and so, with Brian's permission, I agreed to undertake the project which I started in late 2007.

22nd December 1938:

Looked like a good day to be born. Well-known people like J. Arthur Rank, film actress Patricia Hayes, TV presenter James Burke, Dame Peggy Ashcroft, Noel Edmonds, Robin Gibb and the great Italian composer Puccini were all born on this day.

Brian's words:

It was snowing and a very cold evening at 29 Mount Drive Bedworth, near Coventry in Warwickshire, UK on 22nd December 1938. At home that evening Margaret Christina (Madge) Locking was giving birth to a baby, and her sister Mabel Barnsley was preparing to assist her with her imminent birth... ME!

As I was reliably informed years later, after my immediate birth, I was "blue" and not breathing so my Auntie Mabel promptly picked me up and slapped me firmly on my bum to make me breathe, and I was a hefty 10lb baby!

They named me Brian Geoffrey Locking and I was the second son of Margaret Christina (Madge) and Herbert (Bob) Locking. My brother John Robert was born earlier in 1934.

At the time of birth, Bedworth was noted for coal mining and limestone. Nearby Coventry had an airfield which later became the home for the Dakota aircraft. The Dakota aeroplane was unlike any modern jet aircraft today. It had no nose wheels but parked only on a small tail wheel with its nose in the air. You had to duck your head to get through the door of the aircraft, and then walk up the sloping floor to get to your seat. Unlike a jet aircraft, the acceleration was gentle, but there was a growling roar as the engines revved up and the propellers spun round. There was a lot of noise and vibration from the engines.

Records show that over 12,000 were made. The aircraft first flew around 1935 but had to stop flying passengers in 2008 because of EU safety regulation. A Dakota was seen flying in the James Bond film *Quantum of Solace*, when Daniel Craig played the part of 007 James Bond, and the aircraft was used extensively during the Second World War.

How am I so knowledgeable about this aircraft? Well, when I was with Marty Wilde and the Wildcats, we flew across the English Channel to Guernsey in a Dakota aircraft in 1959, and "Dakota" was of course also the instrumental number I had recorded with the Shadows in August 1962.

Mum and Dad with Robert and Brian (on Mum's knee)

Auntie Mabel, Brian and Mum

CHILDHOOD

Brian's words:

My first memories I personally remember were when we moved to Grantham in Lincolnshire, UK in 1939 because of the Second World War situation. My dad obtained an important job there as a grinder at a UK-based firm that designed and produced defence products, particularly aircraft cannon and naval anti-aircraft cannon. This firm was called BMARC (British Manufacture and Research Company), or, commonly known to the people in Grantham as Marco's.

My father also had family living in Grantham: his parents Arthur and Clara, and his four sisters, Mary, Annie, Freda and Nellie.

We first lived in a tiny, terraced house in Sexton's Row Grantham, then moved into a slightly larger terraced house just around the corner, at No5 Witham Place. This was a little street not far from the main river which ran through Grantham and had a little bridge over it at the top of the street. Witham Place would occasionally get flooded when the river got high. Also, the street had ONE gas lamp for lighting the whole street (there were terraced houses either side of the street).

Our house had a communal backyard which was shared by six houses and families, and these included my grandmother and grandad Clara and Arthur Locking, my auntie Freda and uncle George Bradshaw, and my auntie Nellie and uncle Albert Money, and, of course, my cousins Gerald Money and Arthur Bradshaw.

The house had no electricity and we used gas mantles with a taper. Of course, we had no TV, washing machines or fridges etc. Entertainment was a Cossor radio that whistled and hummed when you tuned the tuning dial and was powered by two accumulator batteries which had to be recharged weekly then re-clipped into the back of the radio. I used to collect these from the store on my way back from school.

As the Second World War was still in progress, we had, at the bottom of our yard, an air-raid shelter, where we used to evacuate to when enemy fighter aircraft came into the area.

I can recall on 24th October 1942, being huddled in that smelly shelter, listening to the drone of enemy aircraft going overhead. Suddenly everything went quiet as the engines were turned off and the propellors stopped turning, during the next minute there was a rattle, whistle and huge explosion as bombs hit buildings!

When we eventually came out of the shelter half of the houses in nearby St Anne's Street and most of Stuart Street (including their air-raid shelters), had been extensively damaged by the enemy bombers. Tragically, 30 people had lost their lives during that air raid.

My brother Robert was due that night to have a sleepover with his friend who lived in Stuart Street, but because Robert had done something naughty, our mum, as punishment, forbade him to see his friend. His friend and his family were all killed by the bomb that night!!

Wartime children like me had lots of excitement at this time. I regularly used to talk to the prisoners of war who were repairing the road in the Grantham area. I knew they talked in a "funny way", but I was too young to realise they were speaking with a German accent.

I can remember one day playing near to where they were working, when I managed to get my head stuck between some iron railings on a bridge. Try as I could, I was unable to free myself, and eventually a German prisoner of war person came over and managed to release me from the railings!

There was a wonderful communal spirit that existed there, and they were very happy days for me and my cousins and all the kids in the street, including Geoff Ellis, John Capon, Kathleen and Shirley Topham, Chick Fowler, Brian Church, and many more...

Close to where I lived there were three rival gangs in Edward Street, Stuart Street and St Anne's Street. It was mostly friendly rivalry, except when it came to throwing stones at each other!

In Dysart Park, near to where we lived, we would put our coats down on the grass to make goal posts and play football. It didn't matter then which street gang you belonged to, you were just in! We just got together and played the game, kicking our hefty, heavy football all afternoon.

I was a member of St Anne's Street gang. We regularly played hide and seek and rode our bikes on the dirt track we created from the bombed building sites, and we would play in the bomb craters in the field just outside of Grantham. These deep craters provided great playing areas. On 5th November, firework night, the traditional bonfire was always held on the St Anne's Street bombed site.

Our passageway to our communal yard in Witham Place was a great area for bouncing our small and heavy rubber balls off the passage wall. They really bounced hard all around and made a great sound! When I went back and visited Witham Place many years later, just before the houses were demolished, I was thrilled to see the ball marks were still there to be seen on the passage walls!!

At the little bridge over the river from our street, we would take our jam jars and drop them quickly into the river, wait a few moments, then pull them up quickly. We could easily catch four or five fish in a jar at one time and caught many minnows and reddies. It was so exciting!

They were happy days for me. Another most exciting pastime was sitting in the large archway, opposite side to my house, (which led to other houses with a shared yard), with my cousins and friends. We would read comics, *Dan Dare*, *The Beano*, *The Hotspur* and The *Dandy* which I used to fetch from our friend Rodney Humphrey's mum in Sextons Row every weekend after Rodney had finished with them, then we would pass them around. Great times!!

Those days were always happy and whilst we were in gangs and sometimes mischievous, we never created any serious problems for anyone.

Witham Place (after flooding)

Brian's friends and playmates (in Witham Place communal yard)

Our Brian

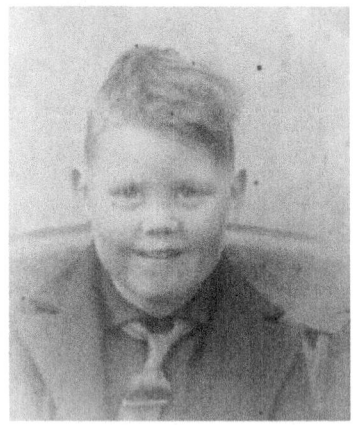

Bomb devastation in nearby street.

SCHOOL DAYS

Brian's words:

I was five years old when I started at St Anne's Primary School before moving up to Spitalgate School and finally spending my senior years at Huntingtower Road School.

In 1944, my mum took me for my first day at school. I was wearing my balaclava hat and I took my red wooden train that my dad had made for me.

My first teacher was a Miss White, and she looked at me and said, "How are you today, Brian?" I replied with a silly comment saying, "I'm fine today but do you know what I did yesterday?" "No", she said, "what did you do?" "I broke my neck!" I said! What she thought of me I'll never know!!

I remember doing a little four-piece puzzle on my first day and on my second day, one of the other boys was picking on me and annoying me, so I picked a fight with him in the playground and banged his head against a brick wall. He never bothered me again!

I still have my first ever school exercise book. Written across it is "Jack Spratt could no fat".

My eldest brother Robert went to the same school as me at primary school, and he was in the top class. He was always bright and clever, and he passed his eleven-plus exam to go on to the top school in Grantham, The King's Grammar School, which is well known for having famous scholars, the most notable attending there between 1655 and 1660, Sir Isaac Newton, (he invented gravity), and his signature is still seen carved on the school wall. Other scholars included Captain Albert Ball, VC DSO MC (First World War flying ace), Nicholas Parsons (actor and TV personality, and Air Vice Marshall Gary Waterfall, CBE (senior RAF Officer Chief of Staff (operations) Permanent Joint Headquarters).

Robert was in his element there and made great achievements in the fields of education and sport, especially swimming, and became a school champion and head boy.

I disliked school and didn't do very well at all. I was more interested in being with my friends and cousins, and never really tried with my work. I took my eleven-plus but failed and went to Spitalgate Secondary Modern School at 11 years of age, and I was still wearing short trousers!

I alternated between the two bottom classes, A and B. Because I was "bottom of the whole school", when I got my school report, I decided to throw it in the River Witham on my way home, and I told Mum and Dad that I had lost it!

But I was a slow learner and gradually improved, and in my next exam in Mr Smith's class, I became seventh highest in the school and in my last year, I became second highest, WOO HOO!!

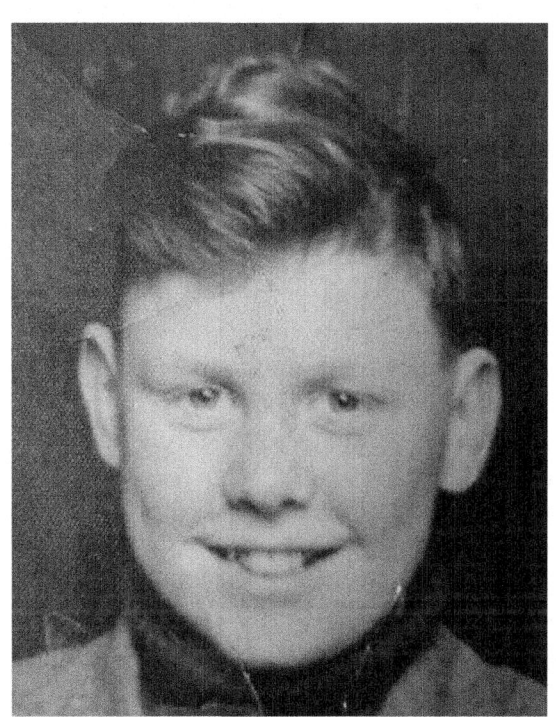

Our Brian

ADOLESCENCE

Brian's words:

In 1950 at 12 years of age, I still lived in Witham Place and that year, my mum was expecting a baby, and on 6th May the baby was born at Hill View Maternity Hospital in Grantham.

When I came home from school at 4pm, I remember running all the way home and was very excited to see a wonderful baby girl sleeping in a cot. There she was fast asleep, and I put my hand into hers and she gripped my little finger tightly, and what a beautiful moment that was, I shall never forget it. My mum and dad named her Barbara.

I had always wanted a sister, and wanted her to be left-handed, and to have blue eyes like me, but when I put an item into her left hand, she would immediately put it into her right hand... and her eyes turned out to be brown, just like my mum's. BUT she did turn out to have red hair like my mum and me and my grandma (Mum's mum).

Although I was not always interested in school lessons, I had developed an enthusiasm for music and when I was eight years old, I joined Grantham's brass band. The Grantham Town Band was a good starting ground for many local musicians, including me. I played the euphonium first then moved on to a flugel horn. I enjoyed it for a while then I lost interest in brass band music.

When I was 15 years old, I rediscovered music again. My sister Barbara was now three years old, and my mum had just bought her a yellow plastic mouth organ. I picked it up and tried it. I found that all the notes worked, all I had to do was "blow and suck, blow and suck", but no tune came out!

Then I remembered the "Trumpet Voluntary" music which I had heard played in the brass band, and at my school played by one of my schoolteachers, so I took Barbara's mouth organ to school, and in the playing field, I tried to play the "Trumpet Voluntary", which only included two notes "blow and suck", and I played it and got a tune out of it. It felt great! Mind you, it was all I could play for days on end, much to everyone's annoyance probably!

I used to put shows on in my mum's wash house. I would put up some sort of curtain across the door, and my friend Geoff Ellis used to help me with the show. The other kids used to sit on chairs which were arranged like a small theatre, and I used to perform a one person show for my friends. My first taste of show business!

My school pal throughout my school days was Chick Fowler, and I can recall some of my schoolteachers' names from Spitalgate School: Mr Pacey, Mr Smith, Mr Gathercole, Mr Mitcham, Bob Jealous and would you believe it, I even had a teacher called Mr Marvin! Was that an omen?

My best subjects at school were English and drama. I was picked to play a part in the school pageant. Local history has it that in 1811 the English boxing champion Tom Cribb had a fight with a Frenchman called Moleneax at the Ram Jam Inn just outside of Grantham. Tom Cribb's fanatical manager was a guy called Captain Berkley who trained him for the fight. I played the part of Captain Berkley in the school pageant. (If you are driving on the A1 Road near Grantham, you will notice the Ram Jam Inn is still there.)

On the sports field I was good at athletics in the 800 metres and the high jump. I was the "Seb Coe" of Grantham. I was also quite good at swimming too and regularly swam at the Dysart Park and Wyndham Park open-air pools, and was selected to represent Grantham in swimming galas, and I played water polo.

During my sporting days at school, I never actually won an event but often managed to come in second place.

I also played table tennis at Spitalgate School after school hours. The head of the school was a keen table tennis player, and the school acquired a foldaway table tennis table. I used to help put it away in the cupboard. One day I was carrying the table all by myself out of the building, when I knocked over a foam fire extinguisher. The fire extinguisher activated, sending foam everywhere. Yes, I was a bit clumsy – even now!

I used to bike everywhere too, until one day I wasn't looking where I was going, and I cycled full pelt into the back of a parked car and completely went flying over it. I was out of action for a few weeks with a fractured arm!!

Schooldays in Grantham were good for me although by the time I had left I would have been caned about eight times for foolish behaviour.

I can recall striking a match in the classroom and my teacher Bob Jealous, saw the flame and smoke. I got two strokes of the cane for that stupid action!

Another time a teacher came round and spotted me banging on a cloakroom door, and I was unaware that it led to a classroom on the other side. The teacher there, in anger, took his shoe off and beat me with it all around the cloakroom, washbasins, and in front of all the other pupils. Each syllable he said was accompanied by a hit with his shoe. "Who – do – you – think – you – are – you – silly – boy – and – what – on – earth – do – you – think – you – are – doing?" This resulted in 21 hits on me with his shoe!

Around that time, I went to the local youth centre in town, where I met and made a friend in Roy Clarke, and we used to play table tennis etc. I found out that he was interested in playing a mouth organ too, but he didn't own one.

On the TV at the time, at about 5pm, there was a children's programme show, and one evening, they had on a guest artist called Larry Adler. He was playing blues music on a harmonica, and it sounded fabulous, and it just blew me away with the music and sound. He had so much feeling and strength of sound. Roy felt just as enthusiastic as me after watching him, so we both came to a decision that we would try to save up and buy a real harmonica each.

There was a music shop in Grantham on Wharf Road, and in the little window of the shop I spotted a beautiful red box, which was open, revealing a shiny blue silk inside lining in which was placed a silver-plated chromatic harmonica, with 12 holes and a button to change the note key. Wow. Pure Magic! Its price was all of £3, which was lot of money then for a 15-year-old.

I was in my last year at school and I managed to get a part–time Saturday job at the local butcher's shop, and it involved me delivering meat on a "meat-bike".

This was a large bike with a frame at the front that held a large basket where wrapped meat was placed, ready for delivery to customers. I delivered all around the Grantham area to customers who had ordered the meat. The shop was owned by J.T. Hall and was situated on the corner of Houghton Road and Bridge End Road. I worked there every Saturday, riding the bike and delivering meat, and I earned 10 shillings a week. Only trouble was, at times there was a particular dog that used to chase me whilst I was riding my bike, but I solved that by throwing an odd sausage at it, and I don't think I ever managed to get found out for doing that!

After several weeks, I had saved enough money to buy the harmonica and Roy, my friend, had also saved up his money. We both went over to the little music shop and bought one each. I remember that the harmonica was wrapped up carefully in lots of layers of paper, with instructions written on them in several different languages.

Musically I really worked hard to get single notes out of my harmonica, and practised playing scales, but I couldn't read music. My first tune I managed to play was "If You Were The Only Girl in The World". I practised everywhere, including in the toilet at the top of our yard where we lived, and all the neighbours could hear me practising! Roy had practised well with his harmonica too, and we decided that we would form a harmonica-playing duo.

Our favourite harmonica heroes were Tommy Reilly, Ronald Chesney, Larry Adler and the Morton Fraser's Harmonica Gang called the Three Monarchs. We practised playing Scottish reels. One of us played the tune whilst the other one played the melody, then vice versa. It sounded really good!

Our mum and me (Babs) outside our house at Witham Place

Our Brian, me (Babs), Nanna Chinn, Dad and Flossie (dog) in Dysart Park, near the bandstand, Bridge End Road, Grantham

Brother Robert, me (Babs) and Brian

OUT ON TOUR

Brian's words:

In 1954 I met Peter Ballam, who was an excellent tenor singer, and he used to entertain and perform in concerts along with his wife Dot. Peter invited me to play in my first ever concert in a dance hall, and I played "Wonderful Wonderful Copenhagen" on my harmonica.

Another concert followed at a Darby and Joan club and they had a nice stage with curtains, but unfortunately, the show turned out to be a total disaster! Whilst playing my harmonica, I totally lost it and forgot some of my number and I tried to compensate for this by talking to the audience, but it didn't go right and I was dying a death, so the organisers decided to close the curtains on me. How embarrassing was that?!

Also, the singer that should have been on the show that evening didn't turn up, so Dot, Peter's wife, tried to save the show by going onto the stage dancing in a hula skirt, and I was backstage, where no one could see me, and singing "She Wears Red Feathers and a Huly-Huly Skirt". The audience seemed to like that, and things improved, thank goodness!

On another show, Peter and I got together as a duo and performed an Al Jolson set. We would "black up" our faces, wear striped pyjamas and sing popular Al Jolson songs. (Al Jolson was an American singer, comedian, an actor and was dubbed as "the world's greatest entertainer". And at the peak of his career he was referred to by critics, as "the king of 'black face'".

His songs included: "My Mammy", "California Here I Come", "You Made Me Love You" and "Sonny Boy". Entertainers would never be allowed to get away with an act like that now!

I then joined a concert party run by a Mr and Mrs Gregory, and I remember playing a concert for the Society of Friends at Grantham Hospital.

At this time, The Empire Variety Theatre in Nottingham, Nottinghamshire, were running a talent discovery show and I was encouraged to go for an audition for the contest. I was dead nervous but excited at the same time. The number I played there on my harmonica was "Happy Days and Lonely Nights". I was thrilled when I learned that I passed the audition and was to play again at the Thursday evening performance, where I won my heat and went on to the final on the Saturday evening. Here I came THIRD and was absolutely thrilled and excited, and I felt so happy coming out of the stage door to be greeted by everyone who was waiting there. I thought then... THIS IS THE LIFE FOR ME!

On returning home, Roy and I were invited to play in our harmonica duo at the Granada Cinema in Grantham every Sunday night, just before the main film was shown, and we would play our Scottish reels. We also entered two more talent competitions, but we never won, though we did come third place once.

HOBBIES AND WORK

Brian's words:

When it was time to leave school in 1953, I did not know what I wanted to do. Grantham was a big industrial town with engineering and mechanical firms, but I wasn't interested in working anywhere like that. My only real interest in the town, apart from playing my harmonica, was the same as many of my friends and lots of other boys in Grantham, which was steam trains and train spotting. I just loved all the huge trains/engines, and all the atmosphere at our local train station, which is on the famous main line from London to Edinburgh, and all the well-known and famous LNER trains would run through Grantham station and the surrounding countryside. It was a train spotter's paradise.

I used to visit as many stations and engine sheds as I could, and my friend, Geoff Ellis, and I would spend days sitting on top of the Peascliffe Tunnel Bridge near Great Gonerby, Grantham. It is a very long tunnel, 968 yards long, and is approximately two miles away from Grantham railway station. We would sit on the bridge, with our train spotting books, and watch the trains picking up speed from Grantham station, up to the tunnel, then read the numbers on the individual trains and write them in our books, before the engines disappeared into the very long black tunnel and pulling a long load of carriages behind them.

The Class A4 streamlined locomotives, known as "Streaks", were designed by Nigel Gresley in 1935, and were regular runners on the main line, and their streamlined design gave them high-speed capability as well as being instantly recognisable. There were 35 of them and were built to haul express passenger trains on the East Coast Main Line from London to Edinburgh and stopping at/or coming through at top speed through Grantham Station.

They all had individual names and became famous to all train enthusiasts all over Britain. The 4468 Mallard holds the world record as the fastest steam locomotive, and this world record was made at Stoke Bank near Barkston, Grantham.

We had "spotted" most of them during our time train spotting, all except for two, *The Empress of India* and *The Union of South Africa.*

Our most memorable and exciting time, sitting on the bridge there at Gonerby, was when we spotted a "Streak" in the distance coming from Grantham Station. As we were watching this A4 storming up powerfully toward us, I suddenly saw, to my ecstatic surprise, the number 60009. It was *The Union of South Africa*! And then it disappeared into the tunnel in a billowing cloud of steam. Wow! What a feeling that was!!

With this background of interest in trains, it led me to consider applying to the railway for my first full time job.

My first job was working on the LNER trainline in Grantham as an apprentice fireman, but first I had to start work as a steam engine cleaner. I was 16 years of age.

On my first day at work, I was supplied with a brand new black hat and blue overalls, but I did not have any black boots, so had to wear my only pair of boots I owned, and they were brown!

I will never forget my first morning, clocking in to work at 9am and meeting three other men/boys in the same position as me. I remember a large burly-looking train engine fireman coming to meet us, with his walking stick, and who supplied us lads with rags, tins filled with paraffin and oil and a scraper! Our first job was to clean a steam engine's huge driving wheels, by removing the dirt with our scrapers, and cleaning and polishing them with the paraffin and oil and rags. Then we went on to clean the engine boiler. What a great dirty job that was! Other jobs included cleaning out the ashpits with shovels and swinging the ash into coal wagons.

I was employed and worked at a Grantham shed, which later became a victim of rail modernisation from the steam to diesel power and the sheds were eventually demolished in 1964.

My work was varied. There were all types of engines needing to be prepared before departure, and these included old steam shunting engines as well as A1s, A2s, A3s and A4s. Preparing the engines in order of We had to make sure they were all prepared by making sure they had adequate coal, water and sand, as well as checking that each engine leaving the shed had a clean boiler and firebox.

I eventually was made up to become a fireman and to work on the footplate of the steam engines. My role was to keep the fire going by shovelling coal into the boiler and making sure the engine had enough steam to power the train for the length of its journey.

My first firing job was with an engine driver called Stan Robinson, on a local goods train. The next day I was given a job on the main line non-stop express train from Grantham to Kings Cross.

I felt good that I had fired the train well enough to reach London and I decided to take a break to reflect on my successful journey with my face black from coal dust and looking like Al Jolson. I was just starting to enjoy a cup of tea when I was called upon to fire the train back to Grantham again. So, I had no time to sit down and reflect on doing such a good job! It was hard work, but I so enjoyed it.

The art of firing the train, was to shovel coal from the tender into the firebox of the boiler, little and often, to prevent damping down the fire and running out of steam, so that the train would reach its destination on time.

Unfortunately, on one journey from Grantham to Newark, the loco DID run out of steam on the main line! On opening the fire door there was no fire, just unburnt coal in the firebox! Fortunately for me the train was on a downhill gradient and so we rolled very slowly downhill into Newark.

I used to get very dirty, but always enjoyed my work. I particularly enjoyed our special breakfasts which we would cook on my shovel (clean one only!): eggs, bacon and sausage. Yummy!

Unfortunately, as happened with my occasional mishaps (??), there was another scary incident. We were approaching Newark Railway Station, and had about a mile to go, so I proceeded to put a few shovel-fulls of coal into the firebox, to give us more steam to get us there... BUT... the shovel slipped out of my hands and went straight into the fire! It was real panic stations. Would we be stuck on the line?? But we carried on regardless, and there was just enough steam left for us to coast very slowly into the station, then the train stopped. Phew, what a relief that was!

In 1956 and seeing no future on the railways, my mum encouraged me to seek employment elsewhere. There was a vacancy at a national high street tailor's shop in Grantham, called Weaver to Wearer. I applied and started work as a sales assistant, which involved selling ready-made suits, menswear, measuring customers for tailor-made suits and making alterations/repairs as required. I was 17 years of age, and I did have a few mishaps whilst working there (surprise?).

I was the only one in the shop when a man came in, in a hurry, asking if I could shorten a pair of trousers for him. "Yes, sir," I said without hesitation (disaster looming)!

Whilst altering them, I was interrupted, and after the distraction I continued with the alteration, BUT I forgot what I had previously done, and I shortened the same trouser leg twice! The man's face was a sight to behold when he saw his trousers had only half a leg!

On another occasion I was measuring my grandmother for a jacket. I measured the jacket length at 29 inches but mistakenly put 39 inches on the order form. When she came into the shop for a fitting the jacket looked like an overcoat on her!

The best mishap though was, when a tall military looking figure of a man came into the shop wearing a thick Harris Tweed jacket with leather buttons. He asked me if I could sew a button on his coat, which had just come off. As no one else was available I agreed to sew his button on. He left the shop with the button sewn on but retuned 20 minutes later with the button in his hand… oops!

Babs' words:

When I was four or five years of age, I remember Brian coming home looking dirty and dishevelled and our mum making sure he cleaned himself properly and changed into clean clothes after work, and before I was allowed to play games with him. I hardly left him alone as he was always such fun to be with, and we would go out for long walks. He always had a good appetite for food too and Mum was a wonderful cook, and always provided us with three large meals a day, plus supper and snacks!

I don't know why he left his work at the train station, but I do remember when he secured a job as a sales assistant at Weaver to Wearer, quite a "posh" menswear shop in Grantham, that supplied made-to-measure gentleman's suits, I always remember him dressing up very smartly for his job. Tremendous!

We had moved from Witham Place then up to No 98 Harrowby Road and our house was situated right in front of the telephone box and post box, and there was long line of tall chestnut trees with the main town Grantham cemetery behind it. At the back of the cemetery were steep grassy hills (Halls Hill) with paths through the countryside at the top leading through fields and countryside and to our famous and popular playground, the Hills and Hollows.

The views from the tops of Halls Hill were magnificent and you could see all over Grantham and other hills behind the town. (The town lies in a hollow.)

Many happy days were spent up there with family and friends, having picnics, playing games, having adventures, sledging in winter, and the cemetery acted as a playground too, even at night! We had no fears!!

The post box straight opposite our house proved very useful for our many letters that we wrote and posted. Next to that was the phone box, and, as we had no phone in the house, it was very useful, and sometimes we would receive calls from it (you just had to wait for it to ring if the kiosk was empty!). Once we received a call from our eldest brother Robert who lived in Hong Kong!

During Brian's adolescence (my childhood) I always had happy and fun times being with him, and we were always very close and loved each other very much.

Our eldest brother lived away from home, at Leicester University, then went on to join the army where he travelled worldwide and spent a long period in Sierra Leone in West Africa.

He met his wonderful wife Sarah, and they would visit us often with their children, and they lived in Hong Kong for many years, where Robert was teaching English in a large boys' school. Later he went on to procure top jobs in various industries and his last prestigious role just before his retirement was the Business Manager at the Royal Hong Kong Jockey Club in Hong Kong.

After retiring he moved back to England and lived in the beautiful south of England. Unfortunately, he passed away a few years ago but the Locking name lives on in their beautiful family of children, grandchildren and great-grandchildren.

Our mum (Madge) sadly passed on in 1977 and our dad (Bob) in 1985.

I remember Brian always being extremely passionate about his music and harmonica playing. When we lived at Harrowby Road, our grandmother (Nanna) Gertrude Chinn (Gertie to all her friends), came over from her home in Warwickshire after her second husband died, and lived with us. Her first husband (our grandad) died tragically in the First World War in France on the Somme battlefield.

She continued to live happily with us for many years, before she fell ill and she moved back to live in Nuneaton, Warwickshire with our mum's sister, auntie Mabel (the same auntie Mabel who slapped Brian on his bum just after being born to make him breathe!!). She and her wonderful husband, uncle Bill, lovingly cared for Nanna before her death, as did their children (our cousins) and families too. As a family we were always very close to our auntie Mabel and uncle Bill Barnsley, and our many cousins in Nuneaton and Bedworth, and had numerous visits and overnight stays there, as they did over here in Lincolnshire.

One funny story that characterised our Brian's personality. Uncle Bill was a fabulous fun-loving man and never got angry, and we all adored him. Our Brian stayed many times over there, and had great fun with our cousins, the youngest one, Michael (Mick), being about Brian's age. They were both fun-loving and very mischievous (in a nice way) and often out playing games.

One evening they were playing with their catapults and Mick hit one of the streetlights, breaking the glass. Mick knew there would be trouble and there would be a policeman coming around to see his parents, and he would get a strict telling-off, so Brian decided that he would take the blame and say that he had done it, as he was only a visitor to Nuneaton, and the policeman might be more lenient, and it would stop Mick from getting deep trouble. So this he did, and Brian did just get a mild rebuke and was told to be more careful in future. But later that night poor Mick felt really guilty about telling a lie and his dad (uncle Bill) was sitting on the stool stoking up the fire when he sensed Mick was feeling upset about something and just said very gently, "What's up me duck?" and the truth of the whole story came out. Then nothing more was said as they had both learned their lessons for the guilt they felt of telling lies.

Nanna was musically talented and loved most music of the time and could play anything she wanted to on the piano. She was self-taught and never had any formal training or knew how to read music, just like our Brian. She adored listening to him play his music and always encouraged him. Brian would play on our piano too, and if not playing, he was always "tapping beats" out of any music he listened to with his huge fingers (he used to call them "plates of meat" or "banana fingers"), on anything that made a noise, wherever he was, much to our mum's annoyance I think at times. But Nanna would always encourage him!

Steam Locomotive with carriages coming in on main platform at Grantham Railway Station

LNER CLASS A4 4468 MALLARD steam locomotive (world speed record for steam locomotives at 127 mph (203 km/h) on 3rd July 1938) on the East Coast Main Line south of Grantham

Steam engine shed at Grantham Railway Station

The Barnsley Family, Nuneaton (Warwickshire). (Middle), Uncle Bill and Auntie Mabel with their children, our cousins (left to right) Rita, Lol, Bill, Truda and Mick

THE VAGABONDS

Brian's words:

After working as a duo for a few months, with Roy Clarke, on our harmonicas, we got together with another Grantham youth by the name of Roy Taylor (later to become well-known vocalist Vince Eager), who also could play a harmonica. The duo then became a trio, and we named ourselves the Harmonica Vagabonds.

The three of us were given the opportunity to perform on Sunday evenings on stage at Grantham's Granada Cinema by the manager Mr Harry ("Uncle Harry") Sanders.

We decided to wear some rather "flashy" shirts, and to make them "flashier", the three of us at, my mum and dad's house, decided to sew the letters "H.V." in sequins onto our shirts. We were all very pleased with our needlework efforts until I lifted my shirt off the table and found I had not only sewn the sequins onto the shirt but had sewn the shirt to my mum's tablecloth!! As our musical confidence and ability grew, we entered ourselves for a heat of the then popular *Carroll Lewis Nationwide Search for Stars* talent competition in Skegness. The competition was a bit like the current *Britain's Got Talent* show.

The winner of the heat was Lennie Peters (a blind vocalist) who later teamed up with an attractive female vocalist, actress and dancer Dianne Lee, and they performed as the duo Peters and Lee. They then went on to perform on the then popular television show, Hughie Green's *Opportunity Knocks*, where they released their popular record "Welcome Home".

The Harmonica Vagabonds came a respectable third place, by playing a medley of Scottish reel tunes.

We continued our playing at the local cinema in Grantham prior to the main film being shown, and Uncle Harry always encouraged us, as he did other local musical talent.

One evening at the cinema, Roy Taylor heard Lonnie Donegan's record, "Rock Island Line", being played, and was intrigued and spoke to Uncle Harry about it, and the next day Roy bought the 78 rpm record and played it on his dansette record player. After listening to it, Roy Clarke and I also were hugely impressed with "Skiffle Sound" and we all started to make plans to form a skiffle group.

During this period in the UK (before rock 'n' roll), the music scene was becoming exciting and affecting the hearts of many of our youth, and skiffle was fast becoming the next musical craze. The Harmonica Vagabonds began to disappear as we diverted our efforts into making skiffle music.

Both Roy Clarke and Roy Taylor changed their harmonicas for guitars, and Roy Taylor had a great singing voice! I did try a guitar, but I was useless. The only thing that was my cup of tea was a tea chest bass. Roy Taylor had acquired a tea chest some time before and it had been left untouched.

My cousin "Lol" from Nuneaton, Warwickshire, who was a regular visitor to Grantham, (auntie Mabel's eldest son), spotted it one day and asked me to get a broom handle. So, using my mum's upturned broom, he attached some post office string to it, and putting the broom handle on the upturned tea chest, he started plucking the string and was able to produce some bass notes by moving the broom handle.

I loved playing the tea chest and it had a great sound. The best key was "D" for the song "Puttin' on the Style".

The Harmonica Vagabonds switched their music to become a skiffle group and added a washboard player to the group, John Holt, who was next-door neighbour to Roy Taylor, and had a washboard and wire brushes! (And a van!)

Original line up was:
   Roy Taylor – Guitar/Vocals.
   Roy Clark – Guitar.
   Brian Locking – Tea Chest Bass.
   John Holt – Washboard and Wire Brushes.

In 1956 the group were travelling in John Holt's van to a gig in Skegness, Lincolnshire. We stopped at a café in Boston for a drink, and next door to it was a novelty shop, which sold plastic musical instruments. Roy Clark bought a plastic trumpet, Roy Taylor purchased a plastic saxophone, and I picked up a plastic clarinet. As we continued our journey to Skegness, we were mucking around, and John Holt, who was driving, was pretending he was a compère on a stage and was introducing each of us in turn with our new instruments to play a solo.

After a while Roy Clark and Roy Taylor put their instruments down, but I kept on blowing the plastic clarinet, and John shouted, "Put that licorice stick away!" ("licorice stick" being the nickname for a clarinet).

So, that evening on stage in Skegness at our gig, Roy Taylor introduced me on as "Licorice" Locking, and that name has stayed with me to this day!!

John later left the group and was replaced on drums by Mick Fretwell, and we changed our group name to the Vagabonds Skiffle Group. We became very popular and filled clubs and dance halls in and around Grantham.

We had a regular gig at the *Wednesday Night Hop* at Marco's place in Grantham, which ran successfully for two years. Marco's was the social side of BMARCo, the weapons producer, where my father worked.

The Vagabonds also took part in the Ruston and Hornsby's (another large factory in Grantham, which produced worldwide famous heavy oil engines) pantomime production *Babes in the Wood*. This featured me dressed in tights and knee-length boots, playing my tea chest bass, which had East India Company and 2s 6d (two Shillings and Sixpence) stamped on it.

At that time in the late 1950s, tea was still being imported in large square wooden tea chests and they were the start for most bass players in those days before progressing onto double bass or bass guitar (as funds became available), and being an empty box, the tea chest was also useful for packing other items into it on our gigs.

In 1956 I too changed from a tea chest bass to a double bass. I can remember very well when I first got my hands on my double bass and trying to play the bass part of Gene Vincent's "Be Bop a Lula" in the key of

"C". The thick strings on the double bass tore my soft fingers to ribbons, but with constant playing the skin on my fingertips started to harden.

I didn't realise at the time but playing along to Gene Vincent's record on my new double bass, that a few years later I would be playing "Be Bop a Lula" live on stage at the Royal Albert Hall in London!

The story of Brian's double bass as quoted in the book written by Vince Eager (alias Roy Taylor) – *Rock 'n' Roll Files*

Babs' words:

Roy Taylor who took the lead in vocals and guitar in the Vagabonds, had previously gone through a tough time as a teenager, because he lost his soprano voice via the natural progression of adolescence and was unable to continue with his career as a lead boy soprano in his local church choir, so this led him up to teaming up with Roy Clarke his friend in the YMCA, then going on to meet our Brian and progressing to play the harmonica music, then onto vocals and guitar with the skiffle music. But Roy found he was about to face another tough adventure with Brian's double bass!

In a local paper they saw a double bass for sale at £20 at Rose's music shop, a bargain, but it was in Lincoln, about 24 miles away! Three of the group piled into a telephone box and called the buyer to say that they could afford to buy it. Unfortunately, Brian and Roy Clarke were working, so it was left to Roy Taylor to go over to Lincoln to collect it, BUT he would have to go over on public transport: a scheduled double-decker bus ("Ha ha", that would prove to be fun)!

The journey to Lincoln takes a long time as the main road has lots of bends and curves, and the roads into the many villages on the way, are mostly very narrow with lots of bus stops!!

The journey was made, and Roy Taylor purchased the Bass, but he didn't realise how big it was, and trying to get on the bus with it proved very difficult, especially when the bus conductor was not at all helpful!

Poor Roy had to stand on the platform of the bus and hold on very tight and somehow prevent himself and the instrument from falling over. The journey time was one hour and 20 minutes, and as they travelled around all the tight bends and bumps and curving roads poor Roy's knuckles were white and very painful at the journey's end!

Brian was, however, overjoyed with the bass, and it didn't take him long to master playing it. He couldn't read music, but he could play along with the beat and rhythm. Brian had recently been to see Lonnie Donegan and his skiffle group at the De Montfort Hall in Leicester, and he was soon emulating Lonnie's bass player, Micky Ashman.

The playing of the bass was excellent, but not so good for the poor taxi drivers in town who transported Brian and Bass to different houses/venues to practice, and the support spike situated on the bottom of the instrument was very sharp and was used to move the instrument around whilst playing. Poor Roy Taylor's dad had wonderful honeycomb-effect flooring on his newly tiled kitchen floor, oops!!

Brian's double bass

Grantham Bus Station

Cartoon of bus conductor, and Roy Taylor on bus with Brian's bass

John Holt, Roy Clarke, Roy Taylor and Brian (The Vagabonds Skiffle Group) complete with tea chest bass!

The Vagabonds entertaining at local club

Marco's Place (BMARCo's social club) on Springfield Road, Grantham

Harry Sanders (Uncle Harry), (second from right, front row), on his retirement as manager of the Grantham Granada Cinema

STARDOM AWAITS

Brian's words:

The popularity of the Vagabonds Skiffle Group gave us the confidence to enter skiffle competitions.

After winning the local and regional heats of the competition, the group won through to the finals of the World Skiffle Championships.

The venue for the championship was to be held at the Locarno Ballroom in Streatham, London. Today this has been converted into Caesar's nightclub, but in those days, it was the home of the BBC's *Come Dancing* programme, and we were told we would be performing on it! Was this the start of us becoming famous? We were to become TV stars, and I was one of them!

So, in November 1957, we boarded the train at Grantham and travelled to London's King's Cross Station.

Roy Clark, Roy Taylor, Mick Fretwell and I set off in search of our musical fortunes.

Our performance with the number "Pick a Ball of Cotton" won us second prize in the finals and prize money of £150. Having won the money, the four of us had a good night out in London, and we went down to the HMV sound studio in Tottenham Court Road where we went into a booth and made our first record, "Pick a Ball of Cotton".

The television performance had a great impact on the four of us, and we decided to stay in London sleeping in the back of our van.

That weekend we made our way to the famous 2i's Coffee Bar in Old Compton Street, in the heart of London's Soho.

We were given the opportunity to play on stage, so we dressed up in the group clothing that we had worn for the television show in Streatham, and we managed to put on a good performance which appeared to go down well with the audience at the 2i's.

A few weeks later, when back in Grantham, I received a telephone call, and our group were offered a residency at the famous 2i's Coffee Bar in London.

After discussing the possibilities with the rest of the group, we agreed to accept the residency, and we made our way back to London with our fathers to meet Paul Lincoln who owned and ran the 2i's.

The offer involved us giving up our daytime jobs in Grantham to become professional entertainers in London. The contract also included a record deal with Decca Records and three appearances on the television show *Six Five Special*.

We found a place to stay, at a hostel in Westbourne Park in London. We thought the place was like a prisoner of war camp, and we nicknamed it "Stalag 17"! It had two rows of bunk beds on either side of the room, and it wasn't comfortable at all, and I don't know how we survived there, but it was the best we could afford at that time.

One day we decided we had put up with it for long enough and agreed to leave. We were playing at the 2i's and faced the prospect of sleeping in the van again, when someone offered us a room at No 12 Elveston Place, South Kensington for just one night. We jumped at the chance, and I finished up staying there for two years.

The Vagabonds being under contract at the 2i's also played at Churchill's nightclub in London under the name of the Gumdrops.

Whilst in residency at the 2i's Coffee Bar, Tommy Steele's (popular and well-known singer and guitarist at the 2i's), manager Larry Parnes booked the Vagabonds for a Sunday night concert in Coventry. Also appearing on the bill was Marty Wilde and Tommy Hicks (Tommy Steele's brother).

It was at this concert that Roy Taylor was offered a separate management deal by Larry Parnes, to become a solo rock 'n' roll performer and upon accepting, he was given his stage name Vince Eager.

The Vagabonds eventually split, and Roy Clarke and Mick Fretwell saw no future in staying in London so decided to leave and return home to Grantham. I decided that I wanted to stay on with the hope of finding work on the London music scene, and so I made my way back to the 2i's Coffee Bar in Soho.

During those years the Vagabonds existed in various forms, as a harmonica duo, a trio, then converting the band to a skiffle group, and I considered we were, without a doubt, the ambassadors of music for our Lincolnshire town of Grantham. From our humble start with Roy Clarke and myself as a duo, playing our harmonicas at the YMCA in Grantham, to coming second at the World Skiffle Championship at the Locarno Streatham, during which we appeared on TV and commenced a resident contract at the 2i's Coffee Bar, I thought we were becoming stars! Paul Lincoln, who owned and managed the 2i's Coffee Bar, was also a wrestler who made regular TV appearances on the ITV's *World of Sport* wrestling programme. He used to appear on TV under the name of Doctor Death, wearing a hood over his head with holes cut out for his eyes, nose and mouth. Our musical experiences over such a short period of time as the Vagabonds must, I feel, have made the biggest impact above all other Grantham groups at the time – and I was so pleased to have been a part of it.

**The vagabonds on the train to London to seek their "stardom":
Brian, Roy Taylor, Roy Clarke and Mick Fretwell**

Vagabonds on BBC TV

The day after the Vagabonds had appeared on television in the World Skiffle Championships they spent part of their winnings on making a demonstration record at the HMV shop in Oxford Street London.

The masters of these records have recently been found and they are being released as a 7" four track vinyl record by ROLLERCOASTER RECORDS as collector's items.

ROLLER COASTER RECORDS PRESENT

Vince Eager & The Vagabonds

Money Honey ~ Be Bop A Lula
Cotton Fields ~ My Dixie Darling

Vince Eager – The Vagabonds   The 2 I's Coffee Bar   1957

BRIAN'S SOLO CAREER

Brian's words:

When the group split up after Larry Parnes had given Roy Taylor a solo contract as a solo singer, and changed his name to Vince Eager, Mick Fretwell and Roy Clarke made the decision to return home to their jobs again, and I really enjoyed staying on in London.

I loved playing at the 2i's, and I used to turn up at the coffee bar and play as much bass as I could with other rock 'n' roll musicians and vocalists.

After two weeks though, I was sitting in my digs, and I decided that I had had enough and was really "low in mood and felt very tired. It was a struggle at times, and I wasn't eating properly! I made the decision then that I too would give it all up and return home... BUT, as I was stood in the 2i's near the juke box, a taxi rolled up outside, and in came the road manager to Wee Willie Harris, who was a vocalist singer, and known as "Britain's wild man of rock 'n' roll". His manager's name was Cockney Henry, and he came into the coffee bar looking for me. He asked where my bass guitar was and asked me to step in and replace the bass player of Terry Dene's backing band the Denes. The bass player had been taken ill and he needed me to step in and play in the band for eight weeks in Glasgow. Wow. What a surprise! Of course, I jumped at this opportunity and decided to take that long journey to Glasgow!

Terry Dene used to be a packer at the HMV record shop in Oxford Street and was spotted singing at the 2i's by impresario Jack Good (he was a British television producer, musical theatre producer, record producer, musician and was responsible for the early popular music shows *Six-Five Special*, *Oh Boy!*, *Boy Meets Girls*, and *Wham* TV series, the first UK teenage music programmes). Terry then went on to form his own backing group and in 1957 had recorded "A White Sports Coat and a Pink Carnation".

As it was Sunday evening and Terry's first concert date was on Monday evening, there was no time to waste, so I collected my double bass from under the stairs at the 2i's and made my way across London to catch the evening mail train to Glasgow.

As there was nowhere to sleep on the train, I slept among the mail bags, which was not at all comfortable, especially when we reached Crewe and more mail bags were thrown in on top of me!

Once I arrived in Glasgow, I managed to find my way to the Glasgow Empire Theatre where I met Terry and the band members. Terry Kennedy on lead guitar, Mick McDonagh on rhythm guitar, with their blonde Hofner President guitars. Clem Cattini was the drummer (who later became one of the original Tornados and played on that famous instrumental recording of Joe Meek's "Telstar").

I completed the group on my double bass, and on that first night I went on stage wearing a royal blue suit which had been made for the original bass player.

The following week, Terry Kennedy invited me to take a train trip up to Largs in Ayrshire to meet a pianist friend of his who was working there in a comedy trio called the Red Peppers, and this is where I first met Brian Bennett.

At the pianist's lodgings, the pianist introduced me to the person sitting on the settee by saying, "Brian

Locking bass player meet Brian Bennett drummer." Brian Bennett was the drummer for the Red Peppers. Brian and I chatted for a long while and we agreed to meet up again in London after Terry Dene's tour.

After the tour I made my way back to the 2i's and Brian Bennett was already there. We played together there alongside Tony Harvey (guitarist) and we formed the backing group for Adam Faith's the Worried Men, on stage at the 2i's. Me and Brian really hit it off together!

We played our first gig together outside of the 2i's. There was a guy called Larry Page (real name Leonard Davies), whose poster picture was on the wall at the 2i's. He was jokingly known as "Larry Page the Teenage Rave". We played at a gig at Shepherd's Bush Empire, and we had to board the underground train with the double bass and drum kit, then carry them around to the theatre!

Larry was better known for his hair colourings and Bruce Welch once described him as the worst singer he had ever heard in his lifetime. Larry had no impact on the music scene, but he did go on to manage the Kinks and the Troggs, and Sonny and Cher during their UK tour.

With Tony Sheridan on lead guitar (who later went to work with the Beatles in Germany), me and Brian became the resident house band at the 2i's under the name of the Tony Sheridan Trio. We rocked the nights away for about £2 a night, just enough to buy us egg and chips around the corner at the café in Denman Street after playing for the evening. We also backed and worked with many other rock musicians at the time on their tour dates.

One evening an American businessman, Joe "Singer" Barbera, visited the café. (Joe was co-founder of the Hanna-Barbera cartoons and was responsible for *Tom and Jerry* and other popular TV cartoons of the day.) Joe was accompanied by another man by the name of Brian Maurice Holden. This Mr Holden was married to Joe's sister, so was Joe's brother-in-law.

The history was that Mr Holden had originally lived in London but at a young age he and his family emigrated to California in America. Mr Holden was a talented singer and loved rock 'n' roll music in the style of Elvis Presley and Gene Vincent, and he was so infatuated with them, he decided to adopt a rockabilly lifestyle and changed his name from Brian Maurice Holden to Vince Taylor. Joe was very impressed with his brother-in-law's talent and thought it would be a good idea to bring him along to London where he would try and launch a professional career for him.

On arriving in London, Joe took his brother-in-law and an American guitarist Bob Friedberg to the 2i's Coffee Bar, as he had read that this appeared to be the centre where young talent would play and was part of the forefront of the rock 'n' roll music culture in Britain. Joe heard me and Brian Bennett playing, and they appeared impressed by what they heard. Joe invited us both to a rehearsal, where, after a successful audition, we made up a backing group and became Vince Taylor's Playboys.

I was just 19 when I joined Vince Taylor's Playboys with Tony Sheridan and Tony Harvey on guitars, Brian Bennett on drums and with me playing bass. It was at this time that I moved my lodgings from Elvaston Place, to just around the corner to 39 Queen's Gate,

South Kensington where I shared an apartment with Vince Taylor, Perry Ford and Brian Bennett.

Each week we would catch a train to Brighton on Saturday mornings, to play a gig, and this is how we built up our experience. Eventually Vince Taylor's manager asked us to record with Vince at London's famous Abbey Road recording studios. We recorded "Right Behind you Baby" and "I Like Love" in one take. In 1958 we made "Brand New Cadillac" and "Pledging My Love" with Joe Moretti on lead guitar, as Tony Sheridan had left the UK and gone over to work in Hamburg, Germany.

In early 1959 it was all happening! It was like an explosion of rock 'n' roll music everywhere and in the UK, ABC Television brought out Jack Good's TV show *Oh Boy*. The show was an instant smash hit and was tele-recorded before a live audience at the Hackney Empire Theatre in London.

During this period there was some incident with Marty Wilde over a week's show at the Chiswick Empire, and Marty was unable to go on stage due to a management dispute, so Vince's manager, Joe Singer, persuaded Larry Parnes to use Vince Taylor and the Playboys to replace Marty and allow the show to go on. So, Vince Taylor and the Playboys, topped the bill for that one night and I was part of the show!

After that, things began to develop much faster with one thing leading on to another, and we were fortunate enough to be asked to take part on the *Oh Boy* TV show which was headlined by many of the big named performers of that era. Names like Johnny Cash, Brenda Lee, Conway Twitty, John Barry Seven, The Dallas Boy, The Vernon Girls, Marty Wilde, Cliff

Richard and Vince Eager, who was of course my old friend from the Vagabonds Skiffle Group.

The song "Brand New Cadillac" became Vince Taylor's greatest ever rockabilly track in 1958.

I played bass on *Oh Boy* for Chris Andrews, who later had a hit with "Yesterday Man" and backed him with "Move it", the song that kickstarted Cliff Richard's career.

As the Playboys, Tony Sheridan, Tony Harvey, Brian Bennett and I also recorded and backed Janice Peters on the second of her singles released in March 1959 with the songs "A Girl Like You" and "You're The One".

Brian Bennett and Brian in London

MARTY WILDE AND THE WILDCATS

Brian's words:

I remember one day Larry Parnes (famous English pop manager and impresario to many major rock stars), came down to the 2i's. He had struck a solo deal with Vince Eager and was building up a stable of rock 'n' roll artistes. He was already managing Gerry Dorsey, Duffy Power, Johnny Gentle, Billy Fury and Marty Wilde. On this occasion, Larry was putting a band together to tour with Marty Wilde, offering the bass position to me with Jim Sullivan and Tony Belcher on Guitars and Brian Bennett on drums. We became the Wildcats and toured with Marty as Marty Wilde and the Wildcats.

We were given a brown Bedford dormobile and were offered the services of a roadie to take us around to venues, but Brian Bennett said, "I'll drive," so he drove us all around Britain in this dormobile van.

We played Sunday night concerts all over the UK as well as performing on TV shows, and we went to Copenhagen in Denmark to perform on a show which also had Anthony Newley as a guest on the show.

I flew across to Guernsey in a Dakota DC8 aircraft when Marty and the Wildcats were performing there. The flight I remember was very uncomfortable and we were all well and truly shook up by the time the aircraft landed.

Brian Bennett and I had a good rapport with each other. I can recall the group being driven by Brian from Cardiff to Birmingham, and he bet me that I couldn't ride on the roof rack on the van through the Welsh winding roads. So, I climbed up and hung on until he decided to stop in a town which was holding a fete! With a little time to spare we stopped but the local police decided our van was not roadworthy and we had to get it fixed before we could move on to Birmingham.

I had always been determined to be faithful to my beloved double bass, despite some other bass players changing theirs for more new and convenient guitars, and I loved the "showmanship" of swinging it around, standing on it, and generally doing almost anything I wanted to do with it.

The writing was on the wall came though when, on loading a van for a journey to a concert with Marty Wilde, they couldn't fit the big bass in, so when I arrived at the concert venue, I was given a quick lesson on the bass guitar by Vince Cooze of the Johnny Wiltshire Trio, and I managed to "master" playing it within a couple of hours.

I did continue to play my big bass though, and it featured on hit records such as Marty's "Teenager in Love" and "Sea of Love", and it was only when Marty and the Wildcats began travelling to distant venues by plane, that Marty took matters into his own hands and purchased a Framus bass guitar for me to play.

Sometimes the Wildcats appeared on the stage and played on our own without Marty, but sometimes, despite rehearsals, things could and did go wrong!

When going on stage the Wildcats were always introduced individually. Brian Bennett would come on first and start playing a drumbeat. Tony Belcher was next playing rhythm guitar, then Big Jim Sullivan playing lead guitar. When they announced "Licorice" Locking on one particular night, I made my entrance from the stage wings, tripped over a wire and disconnected all the stage electrics! YES, I could be a bit clumsy!

Another incident was when we were in Blackpool with Marty Wilde, and Brian Bennett's drum rostrum which was on wheels, came away from its anchorage. The theatre had a sloping stage and Brian passed me, whilst still playing his drums and the rostrum ended up at the front of stage next to the footlights! We then all stopped the number we were playing whilst Brian and his drum kit were moved to the back of the stage again!!

My claim to fame with Marty is on his recording of "Teenager in Love" where the line that goes "Why must I be a Teenager in Love", well, it's not that bit... it's the four Bom, Bom, Bom, Bom bass notes solo that I play just before!

As well as recording "Teenager in Love" with Marty I also recorded "Bad Boy", "Sea of Love", "Teenage Tears" as well as playing bass on his first album entitled *Marty Wilde and The Wildcats*.

REMINISCENCES FROM THE WILDCATS

From an interview with Iain Purdon, fellow musician, 14th March 2014

Brian's words:

There is no such thing as an instant expert. We were young, only 19/20 years old, and we knew very little. But we had the privilege of being able to learn our trade in the thick of it, particularly with Marty, both touring and rehearsing.

We used to buy LPs in the early days. I remember the *Poll Winners* series with Barney Kessel, Oscar Peterson and the Modern Jazz Quartet. We loved the feel of that material and used to listen to them all. Swing numbers. Not just Brian and me, our rhythm guitar player Tony was rather inclined that way as well. So was Big Jim, so that's what gave us, the four of us, a foundation for what was to come.

We didn't spend a lot of time jamming together, it was mainly Brian and myself, absorbing all those swing bass lines and syncopations. We were moved by the same sort of jazz. He was always jazz influenced because, you know, he could swing. It was like a hobby; with hindsight it wasn't really. We were moulding ourselves into the players we were going to be. Brian was way ahead of me, he was always thinking of new things and incorporating little references into his recordings.

We didn't try to put all these jazz influences into the music with Marty, though. We just had to knuckle under; our job was to simplify things and get them right for the material. For example, we were recording "Teenage Tears" with Marty, that's the B side of "Sea of Love", and would you believe it, to get the right sound, Brian sat down in front of the microphone and slapped the rhythm on his knees with his hands. There are no drums on that. Despite all the technology, it just came down to Brian and his knees!

Big Jim (Sullivan) had just bought a Gibson guitar and he was very interested in Chet Atkins. So was Eddie Cochran, a great fan of all that fingerpicking. Jim and Eddie used to sit for a long time together and Eddie showed Jim how to play guitar the Chet Atkins way. Eddie had a big influence on Jim. We later recorded "Trambone" as the Krew Kats, and Jim wrote a number of his own pieces, one of which was called "Peak Hour", which I though was quite brilliant, and I never heard anyone else do it.

We felt we were getting somewhere I think, and it was very nice. We always got a good reaction from the audiences. We weren't arrogant or anything, but we felt honoured because our management at the time appreciated us and we had a good rapport with them.

It wasn't only Marty we backed, we also backed Billy Fury at the head of it, and they involved us heavily in that. That was very good, particularly in Ireland. Nice guy and a very hard worker on stage, you could see he was giving it everything he had. Mind you, we were backing him, and we did push him along (ha ha!).

Brian and Marty Wilde

Marty Wilde & The Wildcats rehearsing on stage at Glasgow Empire, February 1960: Marty Wilde, Licorice Locking, Brian Bennett, Big Jim Sullivan and Tony Belcher.
(Photos: Bob McLoud)

Marty Wilde on tour with the Wildcats (Big Jim Sullivan, Brian Bennett, Tony Belcher and Brian) with their Dakota plane in the background

The Wildcats: Tony Belcher (rhythm guitar), Brian (bass guitar), Brian Bennett (drums) and Big Jim Sullivan (lead guitar)

STORY OF A TILLER GIRL

Babs' words:

The Tiller Girls were among the most popular dance troupes, and John Tiller from Manchester, England, found that by the girls linking arms they could dance as one, and he is credited with inventing the precision dance. The girls were possibly most famous for their high-kicking routines and their fame grew around the world. They would perform in many famous theatres, they were all beautiful, wore fabulous costumes and were skilled dancers.

In 1960, whilst performing in Bournemouth with Marty and the Wildcats, also on the show's bill were the Tiller Girls. Linda Hansen, one of these girls, met Brian when he was appearing as a Wildcat with Marty Wilde and appeared on the same show.

She described herself as being a teenager in her "crush years", and was overwhelmed at being in the Tillers and working with wonderful people.

Linda recalls her first meeting of Brian, "We were in the rehearsal room and Brian had his shoulders 'hunched up' and looked like he had no neck! All us girls felt so sorry for him and genuinely thought that he didn't have a neck!"

Linda developed a teenage crush on Brian but, whilst he regarded her as a good friend, we don't think he knew of her true feelings.

She would accompany him on some of his journeys, and she took a photo of him with his legs wrapped around a pole outside of the stage door!

Brian always had a happy go lucky personality and loved slapstick comedy, as portrayed by great comedians of the day such as Tommy Cooper, Norman Wisdom, Eric Sykes etc. Brian perfected his own "funny little walk" which he called his "Chicken Walk" and would demonstrate it to anyone he saw if he thought it would make them laugh. Often, after being introduced on to the stage, he would walk out of the wings, stick his bottom out and walk onto the stage like a chicken walking. It was so funny!

Linda said she remembered when Brian and fellow band member, Big Jim Sullivan, were moving heavy equipment across the stage and both were acting silly, and Brian was doing his "Chicken Walk". The girls thought this was hilarious.

Linda got in touch with me during Brian's last illness, and we remain friends, though I have never met her, and Brian said he remembered her well. She said she still felt fondness for him 60 years later and would never forget him.

Linda as a Tiller Girl

Linda still looking good!

Brian's "Chicken Walk"

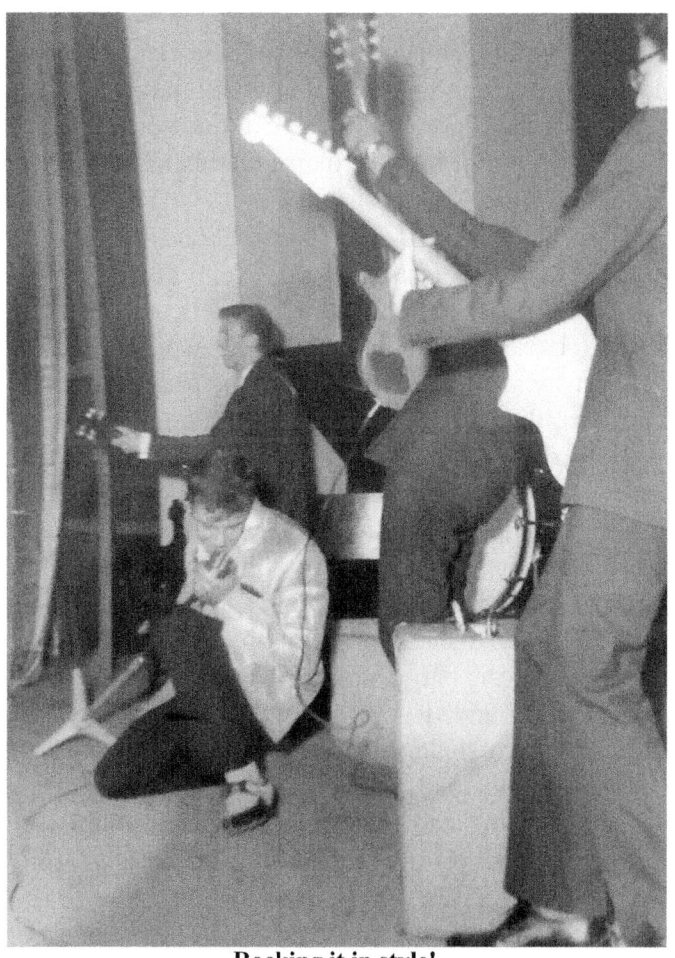

Rocking it in style!

ESCAPADES!

Babs' words:

Another funny story/escapade about Brian, though don't think a certain person would have found it funny!! Brian many times related this story to us and his friends, and it happened around this time (I think), when he was in Marty's band.

Brian, whilst living in London, had borrowed a musical amplifier from a friend, and at this time amps were extremely large and heavy. When he went to return it back to his friend, the only way we he was able to do this was by taking it back to his friend via public transport, that is the London Underground Tube.

He proceeded through London, carrying the amp, until he reached the highest escalator on the Underground. The amp was big and heavy, so he put it down and sat sideways on it whilst on the escalator, and then Brian being the popular figure he was, a friend spotted him and shouted, "Hey up Brian!" and Brian, without thinking, stood up and reached across to shake his friend's hand, when the inevitable happened! By standing up to shake his friend's hand it released the amp which decided to make its own way down the escalator! You can just picture the scene, Brian panicking and trying to catch it whilst screaming "WATCH OUT" to others using the escalator, but to no avail! People on the escalator were diving in all directions to get out of its way as the huge amplifier was rolling toward them, but nothing was going to stop it!! When it reached the bottom it had, in Brian's words "smashed into millions of pieces".

Thankfully, no one was hurt. So, Brian proceeded to pick up all the bits and piled them into a lost property lock up box on the station, then gave the owner of the amp the ticket for the box and told him that he had left the amp in lost property as he couldn't carry it any further. Never heard the outcome of this... but he lived to tell the story!!!

Another incident!

Not sure at what time or who he was with, but it was when Brian and his friends used to travel to gigs in a beat-up style Bedford van, that carried all the group and their instruments, and they travelled many miles.

At this time, they were all travelling from a gig back to London and passed through Grantham, so they all dropped into our house for a cuppa and something to eat. When it was time to say goodbye and continue their trip back to London, it was raining very heavily. Unfortunately, the window wipers had stopped working, so some of the band took the laces out of their shoes and tied them onto the wipers on to the front windscreen window and held the other end of the laces, then proceeded to pull the wipers with the laces backwards and forwards so they could see through the windscreen... all the way back to London in the rain!!

EDDIE COCHRAN/GENE VINCENT

Brian's words:

When we were not working with Marty, Larry Parnes paid the Wildcats a retainer to keep us on his books and used us to back many of the other artistes under his management.

Gene Vincent and Eddie Cochran came over from America for a UK tour in 1960 and Larry Parnes was asked if the Wildcats could work on stage with Eddie Cochran. Eddie had recorded "Summertime Blues" and *"C'mon Everybody"*. We met Eddie and rehearsed in the basement at 44 Gerard Street, London.

On arriving at the rehearsal room, I met Big Jim Sullivan, Brian Bennett and Tony Belcher at the entrance, and we walked down to the cellar where there was a horseshoe shape of five chairs set out in the middle of the room, with Eddie sitting in the middle. In front of him was a guitar case. Eddie stood up and greeted us in a very friendly manner with a firm handshake and a moody smile that immediately put us at our ease.

He then bent over and undid the catches on his guitar case to reveal the most beautiful instrument we'd ever seen. He lifted his beloved Gretsch 6120 out of the case, played a couple of chords, and, resting the guitar on his knee, told us that he enjoyed what he had heard of British rock 'n' roll, but said that it wasn't quite enough! "You guys swing it too much, there's not enough drive," he said.

What happened next was a two-hour lesson from Eddie showing each one of us individually on our separate instruments, the guitar phrases and licks, the drum patterns and the bass riffs, that would improve our rock 'n' roll sound.

Eddie, apart from being an excellent lead guitar player, was also very competent on bass, rhythm guitars, drums and piano. He had been involved in music from an early age, playing in the school band and taught himself to play the blues guitar, and he set about showing each of us how the arrangements to his songs should go. We just stood there in amazement at his versatility, especially when he started the bass pattern for "Summertime Blues".

After watching and hearing Eddie play each part, the Wildcats gradually picked up the arrangements and played the songs in his style. Eddie showed us that by using an unwound third string, the possibility of bending notes was much more enhanced.

We were in absolute awe and have forever been in his debt for the rock 'n' roll masterclass he gave us that day.

Eddie had a songwriting career and recorded several successful records.

Jim Sullivan who used to play a Green Gibson Les Paul guitar had managed to get hold of a double cutaway Cherry red Gibson guitar with a Bigsby Tremolo for the forthcoming tour and the tour commenced January to April 1960.

The first theatre was The Ipswich Gaumont, then continued to: Coventry, Worcester, Bradford, Southampton, Glasgow, Sheffield, Woolwich, Taunton, Leicester, Dundee, Wembley, Stockton, Cardiff, Leeds (two nights), Birmingham, Liverpool, Newcastle, Manchester, Finsbury Park and Bristol.

A typical programme for the Eddie Cochran and Gene Vincent tour was the Tony Sheridan Group to open the show followed by Pye recording group the Viscounts. Then the Wildcats would come on stage with no lighting. Eddie would stand with his back to the audience. When the spotlights were switched on, Eddie would turn round and start playing his beautiful Gretsch guitar which shone brilliantly in the stage lighting. For Eddie's guitar solos he asked me to stand back-to-back with him on stage for a good presentation effect.

Eddie Cochran always performed toward the first half of the show with Gene Vincent coming on stage for the second half.

My Vagabond solo vocalist friend from Grantham, Roy Taylor, alias his stage name "Vince Eager", would often close the first half of the show, and other musical artistes under Larry Parnes' management were interchanged at different venues on the tour.

Because Gene was disabled, he would clutch the microphone and stand in his usual pose with his left injured leg stretched out behind him whilst he sang then, to the audience's surprise, he would suddenly swing his leg (complete with the leg iron brace) over the top of the microphone!

Toward the end of each show Gene would sit down on the stage and sing the slow ballad "Over The Rainbow" before closing with his final number which was always "What'd I Say".

When Gene Vincent wasn't using the Wildcats, he had a group of backing musicians named the Beat Boys, which featured Joe Brown on lead guitar, Tex Makin on bass, Red Reece on drums and Clyde Powell (later to become known as Georgie Fame) on the piano. Georgie Fame would become a recognised name with his band the Blue Flames, and Joe Brown would later front his own group the Bruvvers.

One experience I recall was on the stage of the Birmingham Hippodrome, with Eddie Cochran and Gene Vincent. Usually, after Eddie and the Wildcats had played their session, if Gene Vincent had his own band on stage, I would stand in the wings and watch them perform. So, one night I was stood in the wings waiting to watch Gene's performance when in front of the stage curtain, whilst the compère was starting to announce Gene on stage, I noticed that the drummer was not behind his drum kit, so just as the curtains were opening, I dashed onto stage and played "Be Bop a Lula" for Gene on the drums!

Red Reece, Gene's drummer returned to take his place behind the kit halfway through the number. What an opportunity that was!

Working on the same bill as these guys was one of the biggest highlights of my musical career at that time. Eddie was an excellent lead guitar player and very good looking. Gene was very moody and unpredictable and had a very severe stage appearance with his black leather outfit, but he worked very well on stage despite him having to wear a leg iron.

In 1960 I played with both Gene and Eddie at The Royal Albert Hall in London. It was an experience I shall never forget working with two top American entertainers.

The last time I played with Eddie was at the Astoria at Finsbury Park, London at the beginning of April

1960. We had some photographs taken on this last night before we left to rehearse with Marty Wilde.

Because the Wildcats were taken off the tour to work with Marty, Gene Vincent's backing group the Beat Boys also backed Eddie on his last week at the Bristol Hippodrome, then he was due to be flying off back to America.

Eddie was to be in the USA for ten days then planned to return to the UK for a further ten-week tour. Gene was staying in the UK until September.

We had given Eddie Cochran a shopping list of items to bring back from America including drum sticks and guitar strings. During a day we had been setting up on stage, I happened to get my harmonica out and started playing it. When Eddie heard it, he got his guitar out of its case and joined me playing some blues music together. When we had finished, he said, "Man, the next time I come over we've gotta do something together with that harmonica."

Sadly, on Saturday 16th April 1960, just before midnight, 21-year-old Eddie Cochran was involved in a severe road traffic accident.

Whilst he was in the UK Eddie suffered from homesickness and he was keen to get back to the USA. He had booked a taxi to take him to the airport. Gene Vincent and Eddie's girlfriend Sharon Sheeley went with him. Gene being disabled with his leg iron had to sit in the front of the taxi and Sharon sat in the back. They were in a Ford Consul taxi travelling on the A4 through Chippenham in Wiltshire when the taxi left the road and crashed into a lamp post. All three were taken to hospital in Bath. Gene and Sharon survived the crash, but Eddie died the next morning, during the early hours of Easter Sunday.

I was on my way back to Grantham on that Sunday when I heard the news. I was only 18 and Eddie 21 when we toured but the experience was one I shall never forget. In those few weeks he had taught me so much to improve my bass playing.

One story that I had been told about this accident was that the Ford Consul taxi and the items in the car were impounded by the local police station until an inquest into Eddie's tragic death could be held. It was reported that Dave Harman (Dave from the band Dave Dee Dozy Beaky Mick and Tich) was a young police cadet at that time and taught himself to play guitar on Eddie's impounded Gretsch guitar.

Three times the Wildcats backed Eddie Cochran for the BBC radio show *Parade of the Pops* and Brian Matthews' *Saturday Club*. We also performed with Gene Vincent on the *Saturday Club* radio show. The recordings for all these three shows took place at the BBC's Piccadilly studios. The songs we recorded with Gene were "What'd I Say" and "Milk Cow Blues".

Eddie was not the typical rock 'n' roll star I had been used to working with. He never at any time showed a prima-donna side to him, unlike a lot of the artistes who were performing at that time, and I liked that about him.

Eddie Cochran's posthumous single "Three Steps to Heaven" reached No 1 in British record charts but didn't even make the top 100 in the United States.

Liquorice, Eddie Cochrane, Brian Bennett, Big Jim ~ 1960

Eddie, Brian and
Brian Bennett in
concert

Gene Vincent, Brian and
Brian Bennett in concert

News of Eddie's
tragic road
accident and
very sad death

THE KREW KATS

Brian's words:

When Larry Parnes made Marty Wilde a solo performer, the Wildcats changed their name and continued to perform under our new name the Krew Kats, and in 1961, recorded our own version of American guitarist Chet Atkins' instrumental called "Trambone". Other recordings I made with the Krew Kats were "Peak Hour", "Samovar", "Jack's Good", "The Bat" and a track that was not released called "Jungle Drums".

The Krew Kats also had the opportunity to be session musicians for one of the top leading record producers at that time, Joe Meek. Joe will be remembered for his instrumental recording of "Telstar", featuring Clem Cattini on drums. "Telstar" would also become an album track for the Shadows in later years.

Joe Meek was working with a vocalist called Michael Cox and the Krew Kats were asked to play on a recording session with him in the summer of 1961. We recorded "Sweet Little Sixteen" and "Cover Girl" with Michael Cox but when the record was released the Krew Kats were listed as the Charles Blackwell Orchestra!

As the Krew Kats, we also provided the backing for the B side of a single called "Honey Cause I Love You". Sadly, Joe Meek shot himself on the morning of the anniversary of Buddy Holly's death in February 1967.

In 1961, the Krew Kats were contacted by the Allisons ("Golden Boys" John and Peter), the British winners of the Eurovision Song Contest 1961 with their No 1 hit record "Are you Sure?". They asked us to go on their first tour with them in Britain. The tour included the Royalty Theatre in Chester in March, with various other artistes known at the time, and Colston Hall, Bristol (including Ronnie Carrol of "Runaway" fame), Odeon Theatre, Southend in April, and De Montfort Hall, Leicester in May. We all got on very well together and had some great laughs.

As well as working together in the Tony Sheridan Trio, Vince Taylor and the Playboys, Marty Wilde and the Wildcats and the Krew Kats, drummer Brian Bennett and myself also worked in a pit orchestra at the Windmill Theatre at Great Yarmouth in 1961, where Tommy Steele was topping the bill, and doing a summer season there.

As well as working with the orchestra, Tommy Steele would use Brian and me as his rhythm section on stage. This led to us becoming his backing musicians for his *Sunday Night Concerts* which involved us flying all over the UK in a small eight-seater aircraft in all sorts of weather conditions, rain, fog and storms, and having the time of our lives for an eight-week season.

Working on and off with Marty Wilde also gave me the opportunity to work with other performers. I toured Ireland as bass player to Billy Fury and was one of Adam Faith's group the Worried Men. I also played for a short time alongside Joe Brown, Jim Sullivan and Brian Bennett as one of Johnny Duncan's Grass Boys.

It was halfway through our Tommy Steele tour in October 1961 that Brian Bennett left the Krew Kats.

Tony Meehan was giving up the drum seat and leaving Cliff Richard and the Shadows to concentrate on his record production. Brian Bennett was offered the position as drummer, which he accepted, and I had lost my partner on the stage.

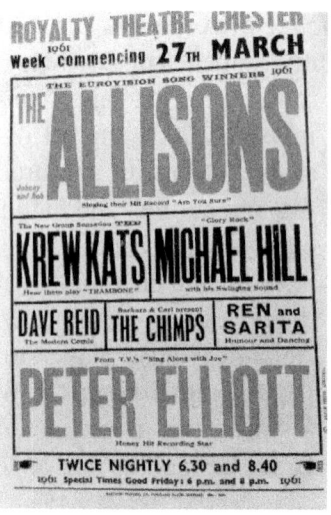

Bob Allison, Brian 'liquorice' Locking & John Allison at the Blue Boar, of M1. on our first Tour April 1961. Vaguely in the background the other Krewcats can be seen - Tony Belcher rythmn guitar, Brian Bennett, drums, Big Jim Sullivan, lead guitar.

Brian 'liquorice' Locking, bass in the Krewcats. In the coach, on the Allisons first Tour April 196 at the Blue Boar cafe on the M1.

Sunday, 23rd April, 1961

THE
BILLY FURY SHOW

Starting Off With A Swing
THE RED PEPPERS
Britain's Brightest Novelty Group
Featuring:
Gordon Webber (drums), Peter Robinson (piano), Barrie Rodney (guitar)

Keyboard Dynamics starring " Mr. Harpsichord "
MICHAEL HILL and his Music
Parlophone Recording Artist

The Most Exciting New Vocal Discovery Of The Decade
MARK WYNTER
Decca's Hit Parade Recording Star

INTERVAL

Hello Again From **THE RED PEPPERS**

The " Teenie Weenie Bikini " Disc Star
PAUL HANFORD
Parlophone Recording Artist

The Instrumental Group Of The Year !
THE KREW KATS
H.M.V. Recording Artists
Featuring:
Jim Sullivan (lead guitar), Tony Belcher (rhythm guitar), Brian Locking (bass), Brian Bennett (drums)

TOP OF THE BILL
THE FABULOUS, THE SENSATIONAL
BILLY FURY
Star of Decca Records

THE QUEEN

Brian Bennett was originally with the Red Peppers Group prior to joining the Wildcats and Krew Kats then toured with Brian and Tommy Steele and went on to become the famous Shadows' drummer.

Gem Windmill Theatre - © Peter Jay

The famous Windmill Theatre in Yarmouth where Brian and Brian Bennett performed with Tommy Steele prior to joining the Shadows

INTO THE SHADOWS

Brian's words:

February 1962 saw the release of "Wonderful Land" for the Shadows. The record stayed at No 1 in the charts for more weeks than any other single record in the 1960s (including those by the Beatles).

It was the start of a new life for me, taking over the bass guitar position for Cliff Richard, and the Shadows from Jet Harris.

In October 1961 Tony Meehan gave up his position as drummer for the Shadows. My friend Brian Bennett was the obvious replacement and because we had worked together so many times in different musical groups, it was Brian who put my name forward as Jet's possible successor with the Shadows.

Brian and I had worked well together for Tony Sheridan, Vince Taylor, Marty Wilde, The Krew Kats, Johnny Duncan, Gene Vincent and Eddie Cochran, Tommy Steele and many other rock 'n' roll artistes in the late 1950s and early 1960s.

I had just finished a pantomime season with Tommy Steele at the Liverpool Empire in January as a pit musician. I did a few weeks work with Adam Faith as part of the Worried Men, and then things started to come to a dead end.

With no prospect of work lined up and nothing much happening to me musically, I had written to my parents letting them know I was fed up and with no sign of future work, I was coming home to Grantham.

I was sat in my lodgings. I hadn't worked for a few weeks and didn't really know what was going to happen to me, when the telephone rang. It was Brian Bennett and after catching up with each other's activities he said, "Jet's leaving," and asked me if I was interested in playing bass guitar for Cliff Richard and the Shadows. Was I interested? You bet I was!

Brian asked me to come over to his home in north London for an audition. So, I turned up with my brown Fender Precision bass guitar and went through "Apache" and a few of the other Shadows standards with Brian Bennett, Hank Marvin and Bruce Welch. I was then asked to leave the room whilst the three of them had a discussion. Eventually it was Bruce who came out and gave me the good news. He just said, "You're in!"

Welcoming the new Shadow

Excerpt from *Photoplay* magazine, 1963

At this time the Shadows was one of the most exciting groups in the world and their simple approach, unmistakeable sound, drive and enthusiasm, made them unbeatable. Cliff Richard said of them "about as perfect as any group can be".

The group started out with Hank Marvin and Bruce Welch, Geordie friends who were at school together, who came to London in April 1958 with two suitcases, guitars, record players and £6 and 10 shillings. They came to London for the final of a talent competition. Hank called himself Marvin after Marvin Rainwater, who had a No 1 hit in this country with "Whole Lotta Woman" and Bruce changed his name by deed poll, reverting to his mother's name for personal reasons. Hank and Marvin were in a group called the Railroders with bass guitarist George Williams, guitarist Eddie Silver and a drummer called Jim, and the reason they came to London was that the group had won local heats in a talent competition and had reached the final. They came third.

Work was scarce, so they began working at the 2i's Coffee Bar, alternating with playing in the basement and working behind the bar. Their job was to operate the orange drinks machine. Hank and Jet Harris were also serving coffee and sweeping up, along with Lionel Bart (who would go on to write some great British pop songs).

Hank and Bruce mixed well with the other musicians at the 2i's and worked and played alongside many of them and met, among many others, Jet Harris, Tony Meehan, Brian Bennett, Cliff Richard (was Harry Webb then), and our Brian.

Cliff Richard was singing and playing guitar on a tour with the Kalin Twins, and he asked Hank Marvin (lead guitarist) and Bruce Welch (rhythm guitarist) to join him, then Cliff could mostly dispense with his guitar on stage. Jet Harris joined him later as bass guitarist. Jet was playing with the Most Brothers prior to this, but he didn't like their music and asked if he could play with Cliff's group for free... the rest is history!!

The group then added Tony Meehan to the group as the drummer and decided to call themselves the Drifters.

They recorded some records with Cliff, but unfortunately, at that time, there was another group who used the same name. They were an American group called the Drifters, and they obtained a successful court injunction on Cliff's band, so preventing Hank, Bruce, Jet and Tony from using the

Drifters name, and all the group's records they had recorded were sadly withdrawn.

They then decided to re-name themselves and called themselves, at Jet's suggestion, the Shadows, and continued to tour with Cliff Richard in Britain, America and Canada, appear on TV and further songs were written and recorded.

The Story of The Shadows – excerpt from book written by Mike Read

After their first tour of America in 1960, Cliff and the Shadows (Hank Marvin, Bruce Welch, Jet Harris and Tony Meehan), commenced a spring tour in Britain where they encountered singer/songwriter Jerry Lordan, and this meeting accelerated their success dramatically. Whilst travelling between town and gigs, Jerry would pass the time picking out tunes on his ukulele, and Jerry played a tune to Hank that he had written, called "Apache", and it sounded so good, that the Shadows decided to record it as an instrumental.

In July 1960 "Apache" was released amid EMI advertisements adorned with drawings of Indians and cowboys with arrows through their hats, yelling "Apache" at the tops of their voices. There was also an advert put out that mimicked a cartoon character from the children's *Beano* comic called "Little Plum – your Redskin Chum". The advert read: "Hold on to your scalps! Here comes the Shadows with their heap big hit 'Apache'."

It was the first of many feathers in their caps and reached the top of the pop charts.

The Shadows group on their own were starting to receive fame in their playing, and would perform by themselves as a group, whilst still working as backing for Cliff Richard. Cliff called this "teamwork".

Their first solo group variety appearance (without Cliff) was on Sunday 25th September 1960 at The Colston Hall in Bristol and was very successful and led on to other appearances on their own as a group.

On 16th April 1962, Cliff and the Shadows headlined the *NMC Poll Winners Concert* at Wembley, all dressed in black tuxedos and white frilled shirts. They played several numbers including "Do you Wanna Dance", "Razzle Dazzle", and numbers from the film *The Young Ones*. The final song was "We Say Yeah".

The original Shadows: Hank Marvin, Bruce Welch, Tony Meehan and Jet Harris

The leaving Shadows Tony Meehan and Jet Harris, who would later form the own duo and make their own records including "Diamonds" and "Scarlett 'O Hara".

The debut for the "new Shadow" Brian.

THE NEW SHADOW

Brian's words:

Well, you could have knocked me down with a puff of wind – it was the greatest thing that had ever happened to me. I'd always been friendly with Hank and Bruce, and, of course, had known Brian Bennett as a close friend for many years, as well as having played with him in various groups, including the Krew Kats, Tommy Steele's backing group, Marty Wilde's Wildcats and touring with Eddie Cochran and Gene Vincent. I'd always admired the Shadows as everything they do is sheer simplicity, methodical, yet at the same one step ahead of anyone else. The fans were extremely kind to me despite Jet's departure, which must have been a real shock to staunch supporters of the group, and they made me feel at home in my new surroundings.

I had stacks of letters in the first few weeks and was particularly delighted by one from an ordinary working family in Liverpool, which welcomed me as a new Shadow and ended simply, "You're all right son!"

It was a great honour to be invited to take over from such a well-liked artist and bass player as Jet, but the fans still had access to his talent via his new material.

So, thanks to Brian Bennett, in April 1962, I was to become bass guitarist for Cliff Richard and the Shadows. I went down to the office at 17 Saville Row in London and met Peter Gormley, Brian Goode and the rest of the management team. I was whisked down to the tailor in Saville Row to be measured for shirts and stage suits. Saville Row was the area in London where the tailors were top of their trade for making suits of quality with prices to match.

Brian's words:

My first performance with the Shadows was at the Queen's Theatre in Blackpool. It was a Sunday evening concert. The suits I had been measured for in Savile Row hadn't arrived, so Bruce lent me a pair of his trousers to go on stage with.

The audience in Blackpool were expecting Jet Harris on stage and a big gasp went up when the curtains opened, and I appeared. The first number on the set list was "Shadoogie". I can recall giving up on the steps and just standing there concentrating on playing the bass parts to this instrumental.

During the performance Bruce Welch (who had always suffered with a touch of asthma) felt unwell and left the stage for three numbers, leaving Hank, Brian Bennett and I on stage to continue the show. What a baptism and start for my first performance with the Shadows!

All my other stage performances were with Cliff Richard and the Shadows. The Shadows used to play the first half of the show dressed in our black stage suits and played the second half of the show with Cliff in our silver suits.

Apart from playing my bass guitar I also brought my harmonicas to the Shadows sound and regularly played a rendition of Acker Bilk's "Stranger on The Shore".

Acker Bilk had his own jazz band and he fronted it playing a clarinet. Being black and thin the clarinet was also known as a "licorice stick". (My own nickname "Licorice" had been given to me by my friend Roy Taylor – later known as Vince Eager – brought about by playing a plastic toy clarinet on our way to Skegness with the Vagabonds skiffle group).

My first harmonica recording with the Shadows was in Blackpool. We were recording some numbers for the French market, and I played on the recording of "J'Attendrai". I also recorded a bluesy type of harmonica instrumental which we simply called "Licorice".

Babs' words:

Looking back, our Brian marvelled at the transformation in his life. Instead of carrying his own equipment from gig to gig and having to find his own accommodation, he was in a world managed by London's Grade Organisation, where road managers looked after everything, and fine hotels were the order of the day. As Brian put it, "all I had to do was turn up and play!"

Sometime during the time of first being in the Shadows group (not sure exactly when), Brian either badly twisted his foot or fractured it, and required it to be in a plaster of Paris cast, until it healed, but he carried on as usual with all his commitments.

Brian told us the story of when, after the plaster cast was removed, he received treatment by a physiotherapist employed at Manchester United Football Club and would visit the club several times.

Brian told us that whilst he was receiving treatment there, he would speak in length to Matt Busby (then manager of United) and the players at that time, including Bobby Charlton, Nobby Stiles etc. They were all great fans of the Shadows music.

(Now this story really set my Dave's heart racing as he was a very avid Man U. fan, and the manager and players of that time were his childhood heroes!)

The Story of The Shadows – excerpt from book by Mike Read

In April 1962, Brian, with Cliff Richard and the Shadows, did an appearance at the British Songwriters Guild charity concert *Our Friends to the Stars*. Also on the bill was Eden Kane, Danny Williams, David Hughes, Ray Ellington, the Countrymen and Max Bygraves. The occasion didn't appear to overawe Brian, and the press described him as "confident and relaxed and came through with flying colours!"

What a time to join the country's top group, when they were top of the charts with their third No 1 record "Wonderful Land", and Cliff Richard was busy getting ready to leave for Athens to make his second movie *Summer Holiday*. (The first one being *The Young Ones*.)

On 23rd April, the Shadows appeared at the Liverpool Empire for one week, and on 29th April appeared at the Embassy Theatre in Peterborough.

The next show after this was the biggie. Cliff Richard and the Shadows played at The London Palladium at the *Royal Command Performance* in the presence of HM The Queen and the Duke of Edinburgh, and it was televised on live TV.

They then continued in shows and recorded at Abbey Road studios, and on 12th May they appeared on the BBC's *Billy Cotton Band Show*.

The next night they were again at the London Palladium and were honoured to receive a Novello award as a team for their outstanding service to British pop music.

Shows and recordings followed in quick succession, then Cliff Richard, the cast of his second film to be made, *Summer Holiday*, (the first film being *The Young Ones*), and the film crew, flew out to Athens in Greece to commence shooting. In the meantime, the Shadows continued with shows and recording until they followed Cliff, and flew out to Greece in June, to take their part in the film.

In 1961, the previous year, the script for *Summer Holiday* was available for reading and Bruce Welch and Brian Bennett were both reading it through, when they decided to give it a go to write a title track for it. Bruce picked up his guitar and began to sing, "We're all going on a summer holiday, no more working for a week or two," then Brian went over to the piano and went straight into, "We're going where the sun shines brightly, we're going where the sea is blue..." and the whole song was finished in 20 minutes!

Babs' words:

Our Brian told us that whilst recording the song "Summer Holiday", it had to be recorded live and "all in one go", so to remember his chord sequence that he had to play, he found a used cigarette packet and wrote the chord sequence on this. He said later, "I wonder how much that cigarette packet would have been worth today as the song is worth a few millions!"

The Dreamer **– Cliff Richard's autobiography book**

Film characters from Cliff's first film *The Young Ones*, Melvyn Hayes and Teddy Green, were to be included in the new film along with new boy Jeremy Bulloch, and of course Cliff Richard. The theme of the film was that they were to be transported to Greece on holiday on a number 9 big red double-decker London bus. They played young mechanics in a bus depot unable to afford plane tickets to Athens, who persuaded their boss to lend them a double-decker bus to drive them from London through France, Switzerland, Austria, Yugoslavia down to Greece.

On the way they met up with three girls who accompanied them on the bus to Athens and in their adventures. One of the girls was portrayed by Una Stubbs, an ex-dancer in Lionel Blair's dance troupe, and she was a great actress with a bubbly personality. She and Cliff became great friends during the film and remained so.

Brian's words:

The Shadows were featured in the film at various places on route to Greece. We were filmed riding bicycles in France wearing French berets, as Cliff overtook us driving the bus and singing "Summer Holiday".

The number plate on the bus was "WLB 99'" and we liked to think that WLB stood for Welch, Locking and Bennett!

Another French scene saw me dancing and prancing about with Cliff to the song "Bachelor Boy" (I'm the one in the white shirt).

The Shadows had been in France playing a concert at the Paris Olympia at that time, so it gave us the opportunity to film the French scenes in the film.

You can also spot me in the closing scenes of the film in Athens dressed in Greek national costume, including the short skirts and those large shoes with the pompoms on them. Hank and Bruce played the Greek bouzoukis, Brian Bennett and I were given tambourines to play and bang on our heads as the four of us were filmed doing the "Shadows Walk" in the main square in Athens playing a Greek-style instrumental version of "Summer Holiday".

I remember we had to be dressed up in our costumes ready to be filmed at 8.30 in the morning. Whilst we were up and ready on time the film crew were not ready for us, so we had to sit around in our costumes, with a St Bernard dog for company all day until we were eventually called at 5.30 in the evening to film these closing scenes.

The summer heat of Athens took its toll on us but waiting around all that time gave Bruce the inspiration to write another Greek-style instrumental for the film which he appropriately called "All Day".

Whilst Cliff was required to be on the film set for eight hours each day, the Shadows were not required for such long periods. One day, to pass the time away we decided to go swimming which proved to be a traumatic day for Bruce Welch. You will remember swimming was something I was very good at in my school years. On this day we were at a house by a lakeside and a few hundred metres from the shore was a raft to sunbathe on. So, we all decided to swim out to it. Bruce not being a strong swimmer got into difficulty and I had to swim over and give him some assistance, keeping his head above the water until we reached safety.

Filming *Summer Holiday* was fun and gave me the chance to go on location in Europe. Not all the scenes were filmed on location. The French nightclub scene where we filmed playing the instrumentals "Round and Round" and "Les Girls" was filmed on a specially constructed set built at Elstree studios in the UK.

Some very good instrumental and vocal songs were composed for the film by the Shadows. Bruce Welch was asked for one more tune and introduced the number "Foot Tapper" into the film.

"Foot Tapper" was originally written by the Shadows for Jacques Tati who was a French mime artiste. Jacques had asked for an instrumental to be written for a film he was due to make. Unfortunately, his film was never completed but fortunately for us it was included in *Summer Holiday* and when the record was released in 1963 it became the fifth No 1 hit for the Shadows. "Foot Tapper" became the closing tune for the Radio 2 programme *Sounds of The 60s*. Other chart-topping tunes from the film were "The Next Time" and "Bachelor Boy" as well as the title song "Summer Holiday".

The Shadows were out in Greece for two weeks, and filming was completed, but it was another year before the film was due for release to the public.

Rock 'n' Roll – book written by Bruce Welch

Whilst the Shadows, were filming *Summer Holiday,* the follow-up single to their previous No 1 hit record

"Wonderful Land" was released on sale to the public. It was "Guitar Tango", and it was originally recorded with Jet Harris, when Hank Marvin specifically bought a Spanish guitar to use on the number, but, for whatever reason, the arrangement didn't sound quite right.

After Jet had left the group, it was recorded again as a single in 1962 with our Brian Locking playing on the track.

Unfortunately, it was released into a barrage of criticism by the press because the style of it sounded different to the usual Shadows playing style, and David Jacobs, the well-known presenter on the BBC Television show *Juke Box Jury*, commented, "I simply don't know what it's all about!" but despite the criticism, the public liked it and it went to No 4 in the pop charts.

Norrie Paramor, record producer for EMI, and the Shadows' record producer, wrote an article in the popular music paper *The New Musical Express* and defended the record by praising the Shadows on their versatility and freshness.

The Story of The Shadows – book written by Mike Reid

After completing the filming of *Summer Holiday*, the boys continued with doing recordings at Abbey Road studios, and playing in shows in Blackpool, Brighton, Oxford, Coventry, Manchester and Bristol, and they were top of the bill. Other artistes appearing in their shows, included Frank Ifield, Bill Pertwee, Suzy

Miller, the Kentones, Chas McDevitt and Shirley Douglas.

On these variety tours, which lasted about a month, Brian Locking was mentioned in a newspaper article which said that, "he had added a versatility to the group that was not present before and he would surprise the audience by changing from his bass guitar to playing his harmonica for a pleasant version of "Stranger On The Shore". In addition to this he also played a jazz-style piece on his bass guitar, called "Nivram".

Brian Bennett did a drum solo with his own composition "Little B", and Hank Marvin and Bruce Welch sang and played "The Young Ones" and "Do You Want to Dance".

Frank Ifield was a supporting act with them, and his songs included his Swiss yodelling song which was his Eurovision entry "Alone Too Long" and his latest disc "I Remember You". Another popular act was the Kentones, and their song was "Softly as I Leave You".

Swisshad 2012 – booklet written for Brian by Heinz M. Rolli

On 31st August 1962, Cliff and the Shadows travelled to Paris in France, for two weeks to perform at the famous Paris Olympia, then returned to Britain to prepare for a seven-night concert tour beginning in London.

Babs' words:

Brian told us a funny incident that happened on stage here whilst playing his harmonica piece "Stranger on the Shore". He was standing in front of the long microphone on the stage, when, as he started playing, the microphone slowly slid down into the floor of the stage, but Brian said he followed it down whilst playing, and ended up lying flat on the floor still playing at the end of song! The audience were in stitches of laughter!!

Cliff, Shadows, Bilk
on Cotton TV show

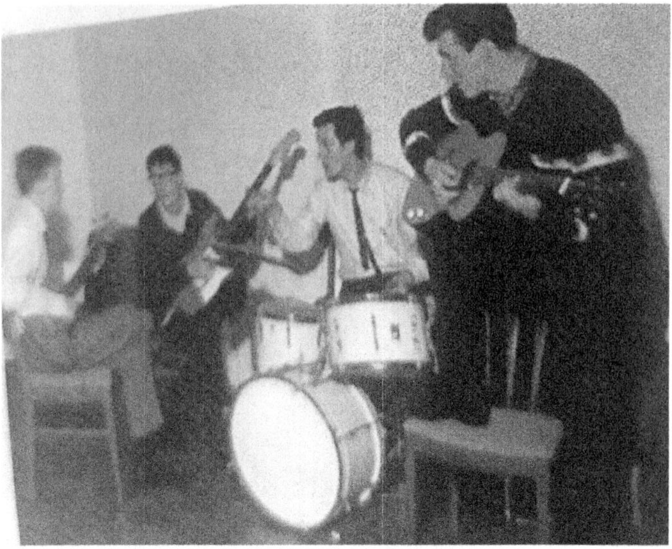

In No. 7 Big Pic of **JOHNNY KIDD and the PIRATES**
· · · POP TEN GROUP & INSTRUMENTAL MAG · · ·
SHADOWS · BEATLES · JET · TONY · JAYWALKERS · PACEMAKERS

BEAT No. 7
MONTHLY

One Shilling & Sixpence Nov., 1963

AMERICAN TOUR

(October 1962)

The Dreamer – **Cliff Richard's autobiography book**

Cliff and the Shads commenced a month's tour in America, to promote their first film *The Young Ones*. Cliff described the tour as having an odd format, as the first half of the evening was a showing of *The Young Ones* (which had been re-titled *Wonderful to be Young* by the Americans, reason unknown), and the second half of the show was a gig performed by them.

Rock 'n' Roll – **book written by Bruce Welch**

At their show in Memphis, Tennessee, they were introduced to Vernon Presley, who came backstage to meet them. Vernon was the father of Elvis Presley. Elvis was aware of Cliff and the Shadows and their success in Great Britain and had really hoped to have had the opportunity to meet them, but he was away filming at the time of the tour.

Vernon invited Cliff and the Shads to visit Elvis's mansion in Graceland. It was described by Bruce as a "mind-boggling experience". Although Elvis was not resident there at the time of their visit, they all had a guided tour of the magnificent colonial southern mansion. There were six garages, all housing different coloured Cadillac cars, one for every day of the week, and inside the mansion, all the floors were covered by very thick plush white carpets everywhere and were magnificently decorated. All was beautiful to see.

They were shown around everywhere and in the music room there was a solitary white grand piano with the initials "E.P." carved in gold on it, and there were also many gold initial carvings in other places too, even on the wrought-iron gates at the entrance to the drive.

They were even allowed into his son's bedroom, where, on his dressing table, was a single picture of Priscilla Beaulieu. She was the girl who was to become his wife in 1967.

One place where they were not allowed to visit though, was Elvis's mother's apartment (Gladys Presley), as the rooms had been locked ever since she had passed away in 1958.

The Dreamer – Cliff Richard's autobiography book

Unfortunately, the timing of this American tour wasn't good, as Cliff and the group and team had arrived there to find American citizens understandably distracted, as the nation thought they were on the verge of a nuclear war with the Soviet Union. Under these circumstances, American citizens were very worried, and reluctant or not bothered about going out to see a rock 'n' roll band from England. For example, in Memphis, Cliff and the band went on stage to find only 200 people in a theatre meant for at least five times that amount. Cliff asked, "Shall I play for you, or would you like to just visit us backstage and have a cup of tea?" This was the case too in the other venues they visited!

Babs' words:

Our Brian said he really loved visiting Memphis, as it was the capital of jazz, and of course, he was a huge jazz fan. He often told us the story of when he and Brian Bennett walked downtown and walked into a club where Brenda Lee was playing. He was thrilled to listen to her and be so close to her and listen to his favourite music.

Graceland mansion in Memphis

ROYAL VARIETY PERFORMANCE

(4th November 1962)

Brian's words:

During my time with the Shadows, I also had the pleasure of playing for Queen Elizabeth II at her *Royal Variety Performance* at the London Palladium.

This annual charity event provides most of the funding for Brinsworth House, a home for retired entertainers. We were invited to perform before Her Majesty the Queen. Other top names on the bill were Australian Frank Ifield and Scottish Andy Stewart.

This *Royal Variety Performance* televised by the BBC was watched by 9.2 million viewers and reached No 1 in the TV ratings... and I was on it!

We had to be at the theatre for most of the day waiting whilst all the acts on the show had completed the dress rehearsals of their performances. There was only a short time between finishing the dress rehearsal and opening the theatre for the invited audience to watch the "live" performance along with the Queen.

When it came to our set "The Shadows", we went on stage first and played "Wonderful Land". Bruce Welch stepped forward to the microphone and politely said, "Thank you very much. And now we'd like to invite you to our vocalist, Cliff Richard!" Then Hank, Bruce, Brian and I backed Cliff on three vocal numbers: "The Young Ones", "At Last" and "Do You Wanna Dance".

At the end of the performance, we all moved to the front of the stage and bowed to the audience, then turned left and bowed to the Queen in the royal box, then once again to the audience before leaving the stage. Backstage after the show all the artistes appearing on it were introduced to the Queen.

With the exception of the *Royal Variety Performance* at the London Palladium, where I played a Fender jazz bass, all my other bass playing was done on my Fender Precision bass guitar.

The *Royal Variety Show* at The London Palladium

TOURS AND RECORDINGS

Brian's words:

As "Cliff and the Shadows" there was a price to pay for being part of this famous musical act. At the end of each of our concert shows, when the curtain came down on our last number, we had to hand our guitars over to the stage crew and leave the theatres immediately, climbing into the back of a van which took us back to our hotels. The fans in the theatres were left shouting for more thinking we were still in the theatre, so there was never much chance to sign autographs or meet the fans who had paid to see our concerts.

As part of the Shadows, I was lucky to be on overseas tours to America, France, South Africa, Spain and Israel.

Swisshead 2012 – booklet written for Brian by Heinz M. Rolli

Between November 1962 and January 1963, on return from America, the Shads continued with recording at Abbey Road studios intermingled with television shows with Cliff Richard including: *ATV Christmas Fayre Show*, *Val Parnell's Sunday Night at the London Palladium*. Radio shows included: BBC's *POP INN* morning show and *Parade of The Pops*. Theatre shows in Doncaster, Bristol, Southampton, Lewisham, Bradford and the *Thank Your Lucky Stars* show.

Records recorded included: "Atlantis", "Geronimo", "Bachelor Boy", "Foot Tapper", "Dance On", "It's Been a Blue Day", "Perfidia" and "The Breeze and I".

THE SHADOWS KNOW!!!
SHINDIG
ATLANTIS

Mirabelle
The Shadows in Gay Paree!

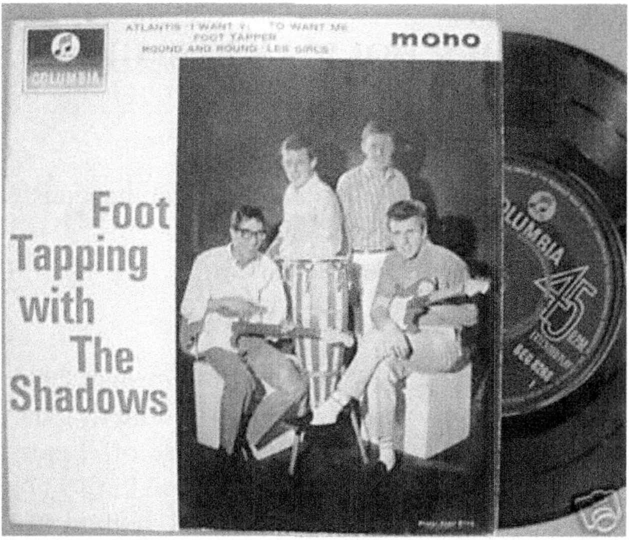
FOOT TAPPER
ROUND AND ROUND · LES GIRLS
mono
COLUMBIA
Foot Tapping with The Shadows

SUMMER HOLIDAY PREMIERES

(January 1963)

Summer Holiday film was released simultaneously in London and South Africa.

Brian's words:

The UK premiere of *Summer Holiday* was held in London at The Warner Theatre (formerly Daly's Theatre) at 3 Cranbourne Street, just off Leicester Square. (Daly's Theatre originally closed in 1937 and Warner Brothers demolished it and built a larger cinema and theatre.)

On the day of the premiere, huge crowds had gathered in Leicester Square. Bruce, Hank, Brian and I arrived in good time and walked down the red carpet into the cinema to watch the film. Thousands of fans had turned up and the police were trying to push them back and keep them under control. The car bringing Cliff Richard to the venue was unable to make its way through the crowd. Although pleading with the police that he was the star of the film, Cliff was unable to attend his own premiere and had to go back to his hotel to watch it on the television.

The film *Summer Holiday* was a big box office success for Cliff and the Shadows, just like their previous 1961 film *The Young Ones*.

Whilst in South Africa, I can remember we had a concert in the arena at Cape Town with Cliff. The Vox amplifiers which had become part of our stage appearance did not arrive, and we had to play this concert with Fender amplifiers.

Swisshad 2012 – booklet written for Brian by Heinz M. Roll

14th January 1963, Cliff and the Shadows embarked on a six-day tour to South Africa for the *Summer Holiday's* film premiere there.

On arriving they were greeted by more than 12,000 South Africans of every race at Malan airport, Cape Town. They were screaming and waving welcome Cliff flags. Police said it was one of the biggest crowds they had ever seen. Cliff, who was prevented by fans from attending the London premiere the week before, told the crowd, "It's great to be here."

Racial differences were forgotten at that time. The response by Cliff's fans was phenomenal. The film was simultaneously shown in four main centres to rave reviews.

Poor Cliff, on the opening night, was almost torn apart as fans flocked around his car preventing him from getting out of the car and he had to be driven off at high speed with about 300 fans chasing the car. On the second night, the police drew a tight cordon around the car, but still fans broke through.

Everywhere Cliff and the Shadows went there were fantastic scenes and crowds. The boys were unaware that apartheid prevented interracial mixing at their concerts and, when this was discovered, they offered to do a second concert for black citizens with the proceeds going to the Salisbury Society for Handicapped Africans.

Story *of The Shadows* – book written by Mike Read

They visited Cape Town, Port Elizabeth, Durban, Johannesburg, as well as Bulawayo and Salisbury in Rhodesia. The charity concert in Nairobi was organised by the Kenyan leader Tom Mboya.

Cliff was criticised by a British national newspaper for commenting on racial affairs, but he defended himself by saying that they went to South Africa to perform and entertain only.

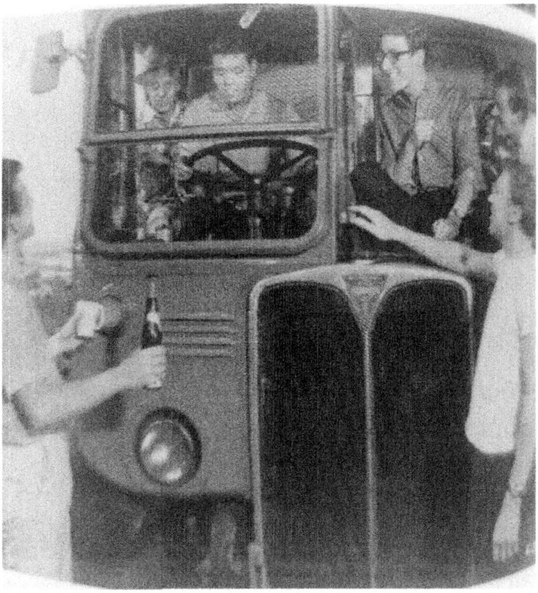

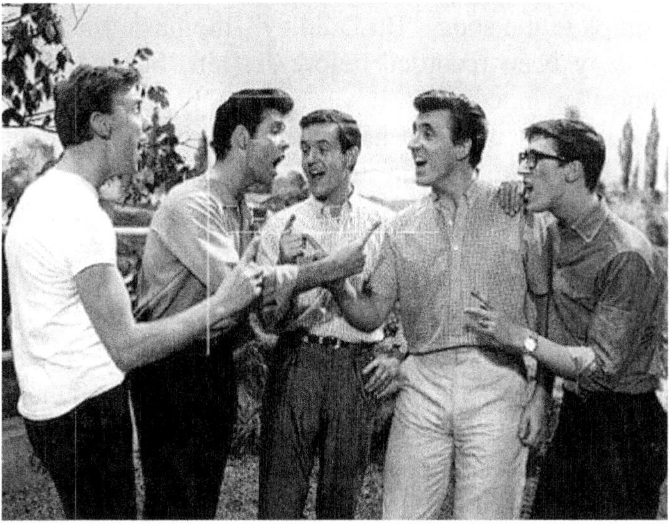

TOURS/RECORDINGS/SHOWS AND LAUGHS

Brian's words:

The Shadows were signed to the Grade Organisation, and I used to travel between UK shows with David Bryce – our road manager.

Most of the recording sessions for the Shadows were booked for the evening. We recorded regularly in the famous Studio 2 at EMI's Abbey Road recording studios in London.

No 2 Abbey Road was originally a 16-room house. In 1929 it was purchased by EMI for conversion into the world's first custom-built recording studio.

I remember on one occasion when we were there to complete the song, "Bo Diddley", the basic track had already been recorded before Jet left, but it had no "intro" planned for it. It was eventually decided that it should start with the harmonica, so the arrangement was sorted out by me in the toilets of EMI's Abbey Road studios! That's the one Shadows track featuring both Jet and me.

Another interesting recording session I had was with our record producer Norrie Paramor. We were at Abbey Road studios recording with Cliff and the Shadows. At the end of the session Norrie asked me to stay back and accompany him on bass whilst he played piano. Norrie had been musical director for the RAF and was EMI's top producer for rock 'n' roll artistes. He had created a series of piano tunes with "fog" in the title and Norrie and I recorded them as a duo at Abbey

Road. One of the titles I remember was, "I'm beginning to see the fog".

Bruce saw to it that the Shadows were very disciplined and rehearsed to perfection on stage, but at times life was not all that serious.

Brian Bennett and I always had a good rapport with each other on and off stage and I can remember rehearsing on stage at a theatre in Liverpool when he turned to me and said, "Telephone." I put down my bass guitar and dashed up the many stairs to the dressing room only to find the telephone was on the hook, silent. I made my way down again and told Brian, "The phone isn't ringing." He replied, "I never said it was. I just said telephone." This was just one of the many pranks Brian used to play on us.

I did manage to get my own back one day. Brian and I had decided to go to the cinema one afternoon and we were ushered into our seats in the middle of the row, halfway down the cinema. The film had already started so we had to get all the other people in the row to stand up whilst we made our way to our seats. Brian was carrying some new shoes he had bought in a parcel, which he put under his seat. After a while we decided to leave as we were not enjoying the film. So, we had to get the people in the row to stand up again as we left.

When we got to the back of cinema I said to Brian, "Where's your parcel?" He went back to his seat, got everybody to stand up again and started searching for it.

I left him for a few minutes and as he couldn't find his parcel, he looked over to me. I was in the aisle waving the parcel in the air at him. He then had to get them all to stand up to let him out again!

Sometimes, when we were performing on stage, just looking across at Brian on drums, he would make us break into laughter. I remember one concert when the four of us came to the microphones to sing "All my Sorrows", Bruce had an acoustic guitar and Brian had a tambourine. I was starting the song on harmonica and just happened to glance across at Brian and I started laughing. Bruce couldn't help himself and he started laughing, then Hank burst out laughing. We stopped the number and we tried to calm ourselves down and I started the number again, but we all burst out in laughter again. In the end we abandoned the number and since that day the Shadows never sang "All my Sorrows" live on stage anymore!

The Story of The Shadows – Mike Reid book

After the South African tour, there were only a few days rest before the start of a six-week British tour. During these few times, the band members would catch up seeing old friends, catch up on the latest records and/or watch favourite TV programmes such as *The Army Game*, *Armchair Theatre*, *Candid Camera*, *77 Sunset Strip*... etc.

By the start of 1963 the Beatles were emerging in Britain, and they had a hit with "Love Me Do" and "Please Please Me", which was also heading up the singles chart. Brian Epstein was their manager, and a very important record dealer in Merseyside, Liverpool.

Brian's words:

When the Shadows were in concert at the Liverpool Empire, Brian Epstein brought along the boys, Paul McCartney, John Lennon, George Harrison and Ringo Starr to watch us play and see how an "established group" dressed themselves on stage.

The Shadows were wearing smart evening-style suits/tuxedos and wearing "dickie bows". Brian Epstein then told the Beatles group that he wanted them to look that good too, and to wear smart suits!

The Beatles met us all and we had great friendship and respect for each other. Paul McCartney would often pop in to see us when we were doing a show near to them, and I liked him as a good friend and fellow musician!

The Story of the Shadows – **Mike Read book**

Bruce Welch decided that to celebrate the Shads' marvellous achievements, he would throw a party at his home and invited his fellow Shads (our Brian, Hank and Brian), Cliff Richard, the Beatles (Paul, George, John and Ringo), and the Vernon Girls (a female singing group from Liverpool, who appeared with many 1950s singers and groups on shows on TV, notably the *Oh Boy!* show which featured many of these popular artistes).

Bruce said that as he did not want to drink alcohol he decided to go into his kitchen to make himself a cup of tea, and when he looked around, the other guests had followed him in!

They all began talking about each other's records and John and Paul started singing "From Me to You", then Hank and Bruce decided to retaliate by giving them a rendition of "Atlantis", followed by a deliberate out-of-tune take-off of "Please Please Me" from Cliff Richard.

They continued singing together, mainly rhythm and blues stuff and some Ray Charles' classics. A good time was had by all, and the party continued until dawn.

Four weeks later Cliff and the Shadows all had the opportunity to fly over to the Olympia in Paris to watch Ray Charles performing in concert. They were all thrilled with the performance and our Brian was amazed to see and listen to the great man himself, as he had always been a huge fan of his. He said that he particularly enjoyed listening to "Hide Nor Hair", "Georgia" and "What'd I Say".

Swisshad 2012 – booklet written for Brian by Heinz M. Rolli

February 1963, the Shadows began a six-week tour of the UK which was strenuous and very busy. They telerecorded for the TV programme *The Billy Cotton Band Show* before commencing theatre shows in: Cardiff, Birmingham, Bristol, Cambridge, Northampton, Romford, Portsmouth, Plymouth, Exeter, Croydon, Kingston upon Thames, Liverpool, Newcastle, Manchester, Huddersfield, Carlisle, Glasgow, Edinburgh, Stockton, Cleethorpes, Chesterfield, Leeds, Leicester, Ipswich (two nights),Dover, Hastings, Southend, Lewisham, Finsbury Park, Coventry, Hull, York, Wolverhampton, Cheltenham, Bournemouth, Brighton … TOUR END.

After this Cliff and the boys went back to Abbey Road studios and recorded "Your Eyes Tell on You" and "It's All in The Game".

The next tour after this on 14th April 1963 was a six-day Scandinavian tour, but just before this, as it was Easter time, Cliff and the boys sent out autographed Easter eggs to many of their fans who were in hospital at this time.

On their return to Britain, they appeared at the *NME (New Musical Express) Poll Winner Concert* at Wembley.

Between 27th April and 1st May 1963 Cliff and the Shads flew over to the EMI Studio in Barcelona and recorded records that appeared on their Spanish albums: *Cliff En Espana*, *Los Shadows*, *A Mis Amigos De España* and *The Best Of The Shadows*.

Brian's words:

During this tour of Spain, we went into Barcelona where we recorded the album *When in Spain* for Cliff, as well as recording the instrumentals: "The Breeze and I", "Valencia", "Adios Muchachos", "Granada" and "Las Tres Carabelas" for the album *Los Shadows*.

Whilst in Spain with Cliff, we decided to spend some time on the beach. So, we went over to Sitges, a coastal resort about 35 kilometres from where we were recording in Barcelona.

One day when we were on the beach four lads from Liverpool (the Beatles) were also on the same beach. I do remember that someone recorded our meeting with a video camera: the Shadows and the Beatles together, but never did see any footage on this!

Swisshead 2012 booklet written for Brian by Heinz M. Rolli

4th May 1963, the Shadows returned to Abbey Road and recorded "I Want You to Want Me".

14th May 1963, Cliff and the Shadows broadcast from the Paris Olympia, topping the bill on the *Europe One* radio show (this was Cliff Richard's debut on *Europe One* radio).

The Story of The Shadows – Mike Read book

After a strenuous forty-two-night tour, on top of radio and TV commitments, our Brian was only too pleased to be in one place for a while. In his own words, "It was great to be able to take our clothes out of a suitcase and LEAVE them out, although there are EIGHT costume changes during a show, so the lazy days were not really any luxury... they were a flipping necessity!"

In June, Cliff and the Shadows commenced a sixteen-week season at Blackpool, but prior to this, on the evening before, prior to the public opening, they were the star attractions at the opening of Blackpool's £400,000 ABC Cinema Theatre, and invited an audience of 2,000 and the Mayor of Blackpool.

Babs' words:

I had just turned 13 years old, and during this time, my mum and dad had taken me to Blackpool for a holiday. I remember it was a scorching hot two weeks.

Of course, Mum and Dad booked a show to see Cliff Richard and the Shadows. I was so excited to see my brother and spend a little time with him between his shows, but of course, our highlight was to watch him perform live on the stage.

We had seen him on the telly but never in a live show with Cliff and the Shadows, (although, when I was nine years old, I had seen him live in a show when he was backing Marty Wilde with the Wildcats. I remember Brian taking me backstage to meet Marty in his dressing room, and I remember how nice he was. I fell in love with him and have loved him ever since!).

We all felt so proud to watch Brian with Cliff and the Shadows on the stage and see how popular he was. It was brilliant!

Another night Brian invited us into his dressing room whilst the show was being performed, and we got to meet Cliff Richard, Arthur Worsley (ventriloquist) and the other Shadows. I had my little autograph book with me and got loads of signatures.

Whilst sitting in the dressing room with my mum, I remember Cliff Richard walking in looking for a pair of trousers from a wardrobe. I think my Mum nearly fell off her chair and almost fainted seeing him in his underpants! He was so lovely though and said something like, "Hi guys, so sorry, please excuse me, but nice to meet you." Our faces must have been a picture!!

After the show Brian took us onto the stage and we met Hank, Bruce and Brian, and it felt amazing and special to be actually standing up there on the stage. Hank played us a tune on the piano, and my mum told him that I was having piano lessons, and he invited me to play, but I was far too shy!

When we returned home to Grantham, I was so excited to tell my friends about our Brian and going to the show and going backstage and meeting everyone.

Brian gave me a load of small pictures of the Shadows, all signed. He said I could give them out to whoever I wanted, so I took them to school to give to my friends. I was at Grantham Central School, on Castlegate (the school moved up to Kitty Briggs Lane in about 1965 and became Walton Girls' School).

I was in the playground showing my friends the pictures and giving them away, when our Headmistress, Miss Hewitt (Nina, we called her behind her back), spotted me and came marching over with a face like thunder (we were all scared of her!).

Her voice boomed out, "And what do you think you are doing?" I told her about my brother and the autographed pictures, but without any hesitation, she proceeded to take the pictures off me and my friends and ripped them into shreds, leaving the fragments in the playground, so that was the end of them!!

She thought pop music was evil and would lead us "vulnerable girls" into "wrong ways"!!!

Another highlight for me, was when the film *Summer Holiday* came to Grantham for its premiere showing at the Granada Cinema, and of course with our Brian appearing in the film with Cliff Richard and the Shadows, it caused great excitement as Brian was very popular in Grantham, as were Cliff Richard and the Shadows.

Mum and Dad and I were invited as special guests to the first night showing by Mr Harry Sanders, the cinema manager, also known as "Uncle Harry", to many younger Saturday morning cinema goers (the "Grantham Granadiers"). Uncle Harry had been responsible for encouraging our Brian in his musical career alongside Roy Taylor (Vince Eager) Roy Clarke and Mick Fretwell, who eventually became the Vagabonds.

A taxi was organised to take us to the cinema and there were photographers taking pictures of us and we were presented with flower, chocolates, and sweets to eat during the film, and we had VIP front seats in the circle. We were really "royalty" that evening!

Mum, Brian, me and Dad at Blackpool Pleasure Beach, when Brian was appearing with Cliff and the Shadows at the ABC Theatre.

London premiere of *Summer Holiday* film

FOR YOUR XMAS READING
ELVIS, CLIFF, SHADOWS
PLUS THE LATEST NEWS OF YOUR TOP DISC STARS
A Merry Xmas
to
All Our Friends
from
K.P.M.
new MUSICAL EXPRESS
WORLD'S LARGEST CIRCULATION OF ANY MUSIC PAPER
—WEEKLY SALES EXCEED 200,000 (MEMBERS OF ABC)
KARL DENVER
PASTURES OF PLENTY
DECCA
The Shadows
The Shadows
with a new charts success!
45-DB4948
Dance On!
COLUMBIA RECORDS

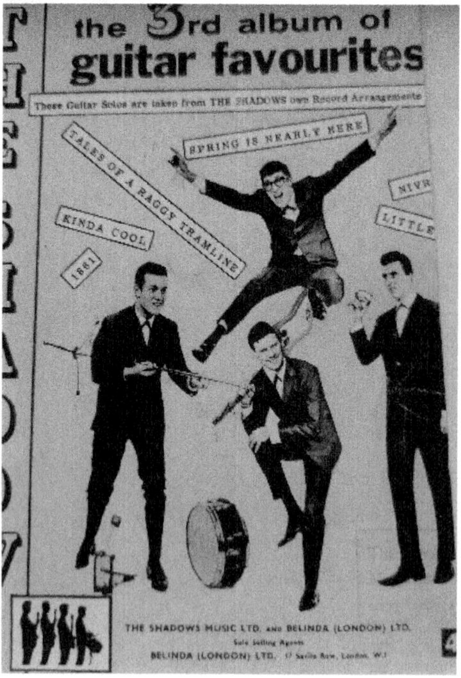
the 3rd album of
guitar favourites
These Guitar Solos are taken from THE SHADOWS own Record Arrangements
TALES OF A RAGGY TRAMLINE
SPRING IS NEARLY HERE
KINDA COOL
1861
THE SHADOWS MUSIC LTD. and BELINDA (LONDON) LTD.
Sole Selling Agents
BELINDA (LONDON) LTD. 17 Savile Row, London, W.1

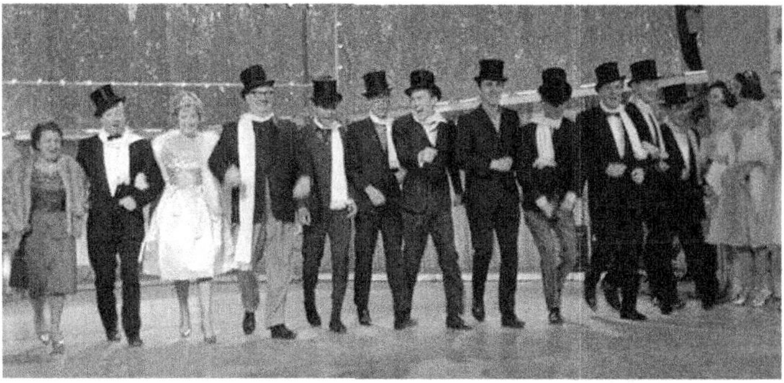

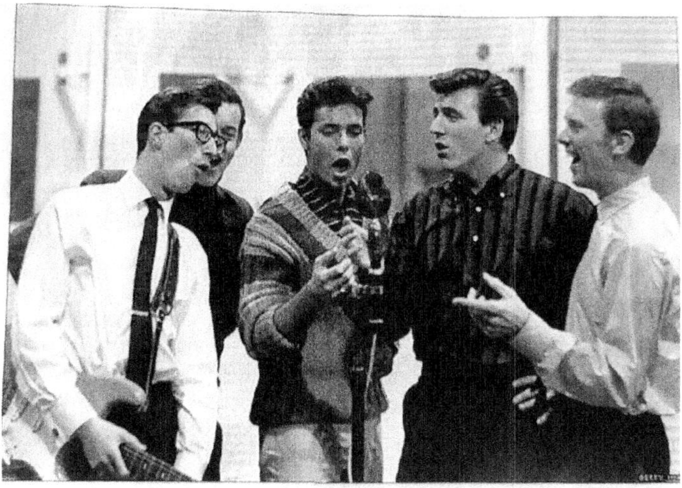

where would CLIFF be without his SHADOWS?

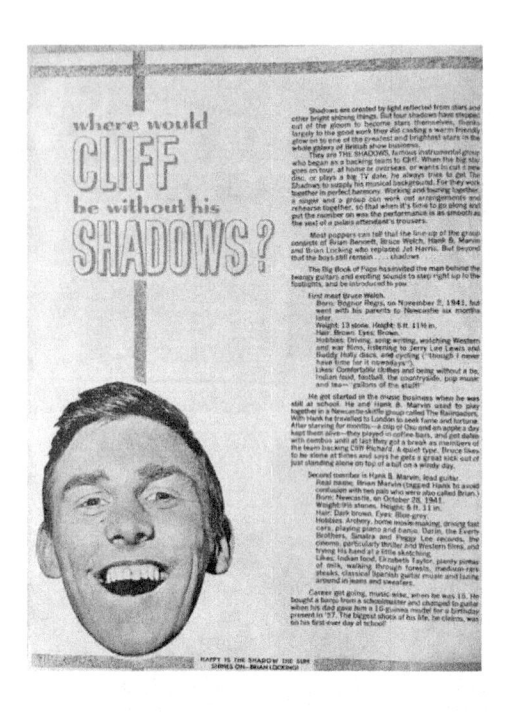

Shadows are created by light reflected from stars and other bright shining things. But four shadows have stepped out of the gloom to become stars themselves, thanks largely to one of the greatest and brightest stars in the whole galaxy of British show business.

They are THE SHADOWS, famous instrumental group who began as a backing team to Cliff. When the big star goes on tour, at home or overseas, or wants to cut a new disc, or plays a big TV date, he always tries to get The Shadows to supply his musical background. For they work together in perfect harmony. Working and touring together, a singer and a group can work out arrangements and rehearse together, so that when it's time to go along and put the number on wax the performance is as smooth as the seat of a polaris attendant's trousers.

Most poppers can tell that the line-up of the group consists of Brian Bennett, Bruce Welch, Hank B. Marvin and Brian Locking who replaced Jet Harris. But beyond that the boys still remain ..... shadows.

The Big Book of Pops has invited the man behind the twangy guitars and exciting sounds to step right up to the footlights, and be introduced to you.

First meet Bruce Welch.
Born: Bognor Regis, on November 2, 1941, but went with his parents to Newcastle six months later.
Weight: 13 stone. Height: 5 ft. 11½ in.
Hair: Brown. Eyes: Brown.
Hobbies: Driving, song-writing, watching Western and war films, listening to Jerry Lee Lewis and Buddy Holly discs, and cycling ("though I never have time for it nowadays").
Likes: Comfortable clothes and being without a tie, Indian food, football, the countryside, pop music and tea— gallons of the stuff!

He got started in the music business when he was still at school. He and Hank B. Marvin used to play together in a Newcastle skiffle group called The Railroaders. With Hank he travelled to London to seek fame and fortune. After starving for months—a cup of Oxo and an apple a day kept them alive—they prayed in coffee-bars, and got date with combos until at last they got a break as members of the team backing Cliff Richard. A quiet type, Bruce likes to be alone at fêtes and says he gets a great kick out of just standing alone on top of a hill on a windy day.

Second member is Hank B. Marvin, lead guitar.
Real name: Brian Marvin (tagged Hank to avoid confusion with two pals who were also called Brian.)
Born: Newcastle, on October 28, 1941.
Weight: 9½ stones. Height: 5 ft. 11 in.
Hair: Dark brown. Eyes: Blue-grey.
Hobbies: Archery, home movie-making, driving fast cars, playing piano and banjo, Tarzan, the Everly Brothers, Sinatra and Peggy Lee records, the cinema, particularly thriller and Western films, and trying his hand at a little sketching.
Likes: Indian food, Elizabeth Taylor, plenty porter of milk, walking through forests, medium-rare steaks, classical Spanish guitar music and loafing around in jeans and sweaters.

Career got going, music-wise, when he was 15. He bought a banjo from a schoolmaster and changed to guitar when his dad gave him a 10-guinea model for a birthday present in '57. The biggest shock of his life, he claims, was on his first ever day at school!

HAPPY IS THE SHADOW THE SUN SHINES ON— BRIAN LOCKING

RELIGION

Bab's words:

Our Brian was born 22nd December 1938, and on 29th January 1939, he was baptised at Bedworth Church of England Parish Church with his "sponsors" (as they were called at the time), these being his auntie Mabel (who saved his life at birth by slapping his back!), her husband, uncle Bill (Barnsley) and our dad Bob (Herbert Locking). The church's belief included "One Lord, One Faith and One Baptism". Our parents would attend church there, along with Brian, his older brother Robert and other relatives who lived nearby in Coventry, Bedworth and Nuneaton.

When Brian was about three or four years of age, our family moved from Bedworth to Grantham, and attended the Methodist (Wesleyan) Chapel on Bridge End Road, Grantham, which was just around the corner from where they lived. (The chapel was founded in 1876 and closed in 1964.) It is now pulled down and no longer in existence, but there is a large Wesleyan Methodist Chapel which was built in 1840 still being used in Finkin Street, Grantham. (It was also the childhood church of Margaret Thatcher, former prime minister of Britain; her parents owned a small grocery shop in town.)

My eldest brother Robert, our Brian and I all attended Sunday school at this small chapel and our highlight of the year, along with all the other Sunday school children, was our outings to Wicksteed Park in Kettering, Northamptonshire. It was a massive parkland with a fabulous assortment of swing, slides, roundabouts etc., and all free to play on for hours on end. Also, there was a paddling pool, and a HUGE water shute, where we all got soaked with our clothes on, and best of all, there was a small steam railway which took us all around the park, through a long tunnel, and around a massive lake, and on the lake there was a large boat that took us across the water. It was so exciting to be there and was a true children's paradise.

Our mum always made sure we said our prayers each night before we went to sleep, and we would recite the Lord's Prayer together.

When Brian left home to go to London, he had a tough time as he had previously led quite a sheltered life and would definitely have been out of his comfort zone!

He was deeply loved and very well cared for by our parents, who would do their utmost to protect him from anything bad, and they would worry constantly that he would stay safe whilst away from home.

I missed him like crazy, as he had always been there for me, and it was like losing him permanently when he went away. My elder brother Robert was away from home too at university, and I felt very lonely.

London would prove to be a huge learning curve and experience for our Brian, and him meeting different types of people he had never known before, and no doubt different cultures, and he had very little money to live on. He always had things done for him at home, so independent living for him would be completely unknown!

Brian's words:

I would like to start by saying at this point in the book that no one persuaded me or forced me to leave the Shaddows. I could have stayed on, but for personal reasons, I felt I had to leave the group when I did.

Being part of the London music scene for over five years and especially during the birth of rock 'n' roll in the UK was a wonderful experience. But during these years I was also a regular attender at Jehovah's Witness meetings.

Way back in 1959 I had started to talk about the Jehovah's Witness ministry to Brian Bennett whilst sitting in another coffee bar in Old Compton Street, called Act One-Scene 1.

Brian Bennett's mother was a Jehovah's Witness, as was Brian for a short time. I was interested but not actively involved. I went back to Brian's home and talked about it with his mum, and she invited me to go to one or two meetings with them, which I enjoyed.

A few years later Cliff Richard also became interested in religion. In October 1962 whilst we were on tour in America, Cliff, Hank and Brian accompanied me to a Jehovah's Witness meeting in Miami. In January 1963 Cliff and Jacqui Irving came along to a meeting in South Africa. Cliff also came to meeting in June 1963 when we were appearing at the ABC Theatre in Blackpool.

My dedication to the Jehovah's Witness faith was becoming more important to me than my musical fame with Cliff Richard and the Shadows, and I was wishing to devote more time to my religious activities.

I mentioned this to my friend Denis George who himself was a drummer and he attended our London meetings. I said to Denis, "I would like to go into the ministry and leave the Shadows." He said, "If you do, stay with the Shadows until all your debts are cleared." So, I continued to work with Cliff and the Shadows until November 1963.

At the time it was a difficult decision to make but I had given it a lot of thought. The Shadows wanted all of me, all the time, yet there was this personal conflict inside me telling me there was something else I needed to do.

Whilst Brian and I were Jehovah's Witnesses, the subject of religion was never brought up or mentioned by either of us whilst we were on the road, in dressing rooms or in hotels. It was always Hank or Cliff that would start the conversation to which we would then respond.

I was on an aircraft coming back from filming *Summer Holiday* in Athens sitting next to Hank. In general conversation he said to me among other things, "What's all this about the religion?" He began to express his opinions, which we discussed, and during some of our concert tours he would want to discuss the topic with me again. Hank always asked the questions, so there was never any need for me to self-promote my religion.

However, in 1962 Cliff and the Shadows were touring in the United States of America. One day we were all sat by the swimming pool of this big hotel in Miami, Florida when someone came over to me and said, "There's someone waiting to see you in the reception area."

Surprised that it was me they wanted to see, and not Cliff, Hank, Bruce or Brian, I went inside the hotel to see who it was. It turned out to be one of the domestic room cleaners who too was a Jehovah's Witness and had seen the green cover of my Bible on the bedside cabinet. She invited me to one of the meetings she was attending. I went, and Hank, Brian and Cliff came too. By this time Hank's brother had also come into the faith, and when Hank married his second wife Carole, he too became a Jehovah's Witness.

So, I made a personal decision to leave the Shadows and follow my religious dedication. I told Bruce at the end of a rehearsal about three months before the news broke. Bruce looked at me in surprise and said, "I've just handed my notice in too!" I couldn't believe it, half of the Shadows giving notice to leave the group on the same day!

Bruce asked me not to say anything but to leave it a while. The Shadows were appearing on TV's *Sunday Night at the London Palladium* on 3rd November 1963. Bruce Forsyth was the compère for the show, and he announced that Bruce Welch would be leaving the Shadows. No one knew that I was leaving too and that this would be the last UK appearance for me.

It was later in the month when we were on our Israel tour, that the news about me leaving reached other members of the Shadows. Brian and Hank were saddened by the news but respected my reasons.

The news became public whilst we were in France, performing at the Paris Olympia for a week. I was suddenly surrounded by reporters. The music press reported that I was leaving, and that John Rostill would be taking over my role on bass guitar.

My appearances at the Paris Olympia with Hank Marvin, Bruce Welch and Brian Bennett were due to be my last as bass guitarist and harmonica player for the Shadows.

Babs' words:

Brian spoke very little about his private and religious lifestyle to us as a family, but all I remembered and cared about, was that he was always pleased to see us all when he returned home for visits, and we were all equally overjoyed. He always came home accompanied with massive bags of clothes that needed washing and always seemed to be hungry. Mum would immediately get his washing done, dried and ironed and neatly packed before his return to London and made sure he ate plenty of his favourite food whilst at home and packed him up as much as she could with food for his train journey back to London. She always worried so much about him, and I was just so pleased to have my brother back again so we could have loads of fun, and he always made me laugh. I absolutely hated it when he had to go back on that train again!

Brian was involved with the Witnesses in Grantham, and they were always very welcoming and great friends to him, and us too. This was a huge relief for our mum, as she knew that they were genuine friends who were completely trustworthy, and who gave our Brian great support. This made her feel happier, and it was a relief that he was involved with these same good people in London.

Brian loved reading and he would avidly read books, and he would study them devotedly. Brian questioned everything, and ensured he knew enough about things before sharing his knowledge with others, but only if they were willing to listen. He always respected other people's personal feelings and beliefs.

The Dreamer – Cliff Richard autobiography book

Cliff Richard was still suffering greatly the loss of his beloved father, who had died in May 1961 aged just 56 years. Cliff was only 20 years old and it and was an incredibly difficult time for him. He had been seriously thinking of an idea of contacting a medium to try and contact his father in the afterlife.

When our Brian joined the Shadows, Cliff liked him, but he did not really know what sort of guy he was, only that he was quiet and studious and kept himself to himself. One day, in a hotel room, Cliff spoke to our Brian about his feelings and his sadness for the loss of his father, and of how he was thinking of finding a medium to talk to his father in the afterlife.

Brian was horrified and told him it was a terrible idea, and did he realise how dangerous this would be, as in the Bible it is expressively forbidden. Cliff was shocked by the strength of Brian's answer and asked him why he believed it. Brian went on to read a passage in Deuteronomy 18:10 and read it aloud to him. Cliff was amazed at Brian's knowledge and asked him further questions about his faith. After this they would have frequent talks about belief and religion in general and Hank Marvin was also intrigued to listen and join in the conversations too.

When they were in Miami, America, our Brian took Cliff and Hank to a Jehovah Witness meeting, and all the congregation welcomed them warmly and the sermons were powerful and dynamic. It was completely different to what he expected, and it "spoke" to Cliff on an intensive level. After the tour, Cliff came home with all sorts of questions in his head and told his mum that he was interested in the Jehovah's Witnesses, and he was totally shocked when she too expressed to him that she too was interested in the same religion. What a coincidence! It turned out that his mum's aunty and uncle, who had just moved back to England from India, had been converted to the faith. This was Cliff's starting point on his spiritual journey.

DEPARTING SHADOW

Rock 'n' Roll – book written by Bruce Welch

During the tour of Israel, when Brian would make his decision to leave the Shadows public, Bruce Welch, who had previously announced he was leaving the group, had decided to reverse his decision. Whilst away in Israel, it gave Bruce a chance to relax and unwind a little and sort out his problems, so when he returned to Britain afterwards, he changed his mind about leaving, and decided that he would carry on playing in the group.

Brian's words:

I stuck to my decision to leave the group, and completely felt that it was the right decision for me, to make and I continued playing up to my final week with Cliff and Shads (October/November 1963).

I decided that I wanted to leave quietly and without any fuss, and so I just left by "sliding out of the back door".

I consider my time playing bass guitar and harmonica for Cliff Richard and the Shadows, although only lasting just under two years, was the best period musically for the group with some memorable record releases which were successfully received by our audiences, and which today over 50 years later they are still popular guitar instrumentals with fans of the Shadows, and are still being played by hundreds of Shadows Clubs' guitarists all over the world. Tunes such as "Dance On", "The Breeze and I", "Atlantis",

"Guitar Tango", "Foot Tapper", and of course "Dakota" were all recorded by me on bass guitar with the Shadows. I also think my harmonica bought a new dimension to the group both on stage and in the recording studios.

Babs' words:

Many people at this time criticised Brian for making this decision and thought it was totally wrong for him to turn his back on his stardom, but I knew, as did our parents, that he did not make the decision lightly and it was for his own happiness and his very strong commitment to his faith, and this we completely understood, and admired his strong stance and loyalty whilst under so much pressure from other people's opinions.

It was hurtful to listen to what people were saying about him, and to us at this time, but we were and always would be very proud of him.

Rock 'n' Roll – Bruce Welch book

The group were then looking for a bass player to replace our Brian and found a lad they had encountered during a Sunday concert engagement at the Queen's Theatre in Blackpool about a year previously. His name being John Rostill, and an extremely talented bass player. He had been playing with a group the Terry Young Six. He was described by Bruce as being a very good-looking guy, and John proved to be a valuable band member with his excellent playing and musical writing skills, which pleased Bruce immensely to have a fellow writer with him, and John also had the skill of tuning guitars, which Bruce often struggled with, and they became great friends.

It was Christmas 1963 when John, joined, and the first performance he ever made with the group was on the movie *Wonderful Life* with Cliff Richard. It was shot on location in the Canary Islands.

Brian's words:

I met John Rostill, who came to Abbey Road, and we had our pictures taken of me handing over my bass guitar to him. Everyone was friendly, nice, and happy with no disagreements at all. I had treasured the time with Cliff and the Shadows and to me it was a golden period.

I didn't realise it at that time, but although it was officially my last performance as part of the Shadows, it would not be my last opportunity to work with Hank, Bruce and Brian.

I was given the opportunity to play bass for them again when the Shadows appeared at The Talk of the Town nightclub in London's Leicester Square in 1968.

The Shadows were contracted to play a few weeks' residency at the club.

Two weeks before the end of their contract, John Rostill was taken ill and hospitalised. I was invited to stand in and play bass guitar for the last two weeks. At the end of my first week, Brian Bennett was also taken ill with appendicitis, and a replacement drummer had to be found quickly.

So, a new Shadows line-up was created for the last week of residency, consisting of Hank Marvin, Bruce

Welch, myself playing bass, and Tony Meehan back playing drums again. It was the first time I had been part of the Shadows since 1963 and I immensely enjoyed these two weeks with them.

Since leaving the Shadows, I have still found time to be on stage with Hank, Bruce and Brian at various other venues.

Rock 'n' Roll – **Bruce Welch book**

The Shadows with John continued to do very well with other tours, gigs and two further films: *Wonderful Life* and *Rhythm and Greens*. Money was flowing in.

Jet Harris, former bass player was doing well with his music, sometimes partnered with ex-drummer Tony Meehan, and sometimes as a solo performer.

In 1964 and 1965 Merseybeat music was emerging with the very popular Beatles at the forefront, and the Rolling Stones were going from strength to strength. The pop charts were being swamped with the different type of music, and groups with a "harder edge" were driving teenagers in Britain head over heels in a frenzy. (Me included but I preferred less "Bluesy" music and more "Popsy" like the Hollies, the Merseybeats, Love Affair, the Searchers, the Dave Clark Five, the Animals etc.) Other groups included were Manfred Mann, The Yardbirds and the Pretty Things etc. followed by the Who, John Mayall's Bluesbreakers and Eric Clapton and Cream... etc., etc.

Handover to new Shadows' bassist John Rostill

John Rostill, happy to be part of the Shadows team.

OUT OF THE SHADOWS

Brian's Words:

In June 1964 the *Daily Mail* national newspaper published an article entitled "Witness Liquorice Returns to Pop". Apart from not spelling my nickname correctly, reporter Robert Bickford incorrectly wrote that I was persuaded back into the music business by a pretty girl singer whose husband was a Jehovah's Witness. In fact, June was married to trumpet player Duncan Campbell from the Ted Heath Band, and it was Duncan that introduced me to June who at the time was working in Clubland with pianist and songwriter Keith Mansfield. June suggested I should form a group and so a band under the name of Licorice Locking Allsorts was formed for music and dancing.

Whilst my work with the Jehovah's Witness ministry was a priority, I still needed to live and earn money so I decided I might as well earn my money doing what I was best at... playing music.

This band was nothing compared to my days with the Shadows, but it was a start to my return to music and I was happy. I had left behind all the hysteria, idolatry and fame working with Cliff Richard and the Shadows.

Back in February 1965 I got onto an Underground tube train and noticed Terry Kennedy sitting in the carriage. He'd been lead guitarist when I worked with Terry Dene in Scotland. As we hadn't seen each other for a few years we fell into conversation. He said he was now a record producer and asked me if I wanted to work with him on a project; he was working in a recording studio in Denmark Street in the basement of Southern Music.

He asked me to play double bass on a recording session with a new up-and-coming artiste with a name I hadn't heard before.

His name was Donovan and the recordings I was to play on were "Catch The Wind", "Mr Tambourine Man", "Colours", and one of the other tracks on his debut album called *What's Bin Did And What's Bin Hid*.

Donovan was a UK artiste who sang in the style of the American singer and songwriter Bob Dylan.

My name is actually mentioned on the back of the album in the credits.

Babs' words:

DONOVAN??!! I just couldn't believe it, that after many years, my brother Brian had just informed me, that he had played alongside my favourite singer and heartthrob of my teenage years! I absolutely ADORED HIM!! and would play his records over and over again.

Brian told me that after he had backed Donovan and Gypsy Dave, Brian thought at that time, that they were going nowhere and he told me that, Gypsy Dave's drumkit was in such a poor state and had been repaired in places with Sellotape!

I always loved Donovan, and his music, and a few years ago I was treated by our friends, who lived in Manchester, and very close friends with Brian (Kev and Brenda Harris), to a one-man show there featuring Donovan.

It was absolutely fabulous to see my hero at such close proximity, and he sounded exactly the same, and told us some great stories about his life and his time with the Beatles. He looked so different though, but I still loved him, and afterwards in the foyer, Donovan was signing autographs, with a long queue of people waiting to meet him.

I thought then, I would have loved to have met him personally and told him about our Brian, but was "too shy", but our friends, Kev and Bren frogmarched me into the queue and said, "You have got to meet him and mention Brian!!"

I felt so nervous of meeting him, but meet him I did! Awww. He looked wonderful even though he had really long hair and looked very hippy-ish!

Dave and I told him how much we had enjoyed his show, then I mentioned Brian, and to my surprise he knew of him almost immediately and said what a nice person he was. Donovan stood up and introduced me to the waiting queue as "Brian 'Licorice' Locking's sister" and told them how he had backed him on his early records. Oooo, I felt 12 feet tall!... and I still love him!! xx

DONOVAN

Dave meeting up with Donovan after a recent show and he recalled his meeting with our Brian and asked to be remembered to him.

New Beginnings

Brian's words:

I lived at various addresses in South London at Herne Hill, Brixton, and Peckham and spent a short time in a hostel in Paddington.

Denis and Pat George, Jehovah's Witnesses' friends of mine, who were also musicians, used to visit me at the hostel and seeing I was going through a rough patch at the time, offered me a room at their home in Streatham.

Denis was a drummer and Pat was the lead guitarist/vocalist for a band called the White Liners. The guitarist was Les Parkinson, and I was invited to join them playing my bass guitar and harmonica.

We played the pubs and clubs in the London area for 14 years. The band played regularly three nights a week as resident musicians at the Downham Tavern in Bromley, Kent. We played Fridays, Saturdays and Sundays.

One evening at the venue one of the customers (unbeknown to us), left a note on the piano. On opening it we found an invitation for the band to go on a talent show. As I had already had my share of fame, we decided not to accept the invitation!

Another evening Liam Gallagher from Oasis was sat near to our drummer Denis George and commented afterwards that we were much too good and should be playing in much better venues!!

When the Shadows appeared in concert in Croydon in the 1980s I went backstage to meet up with them again and wish them well as this tour looked like being their last. Little did I know that their *Final Tour Concert* wouldn't take place until 2004, nearly 20 years later, and I joined them on one of these shows too. Due to commitments, I was unable to join them on other shows of the *Final Tour*, but Mark Griffiths was excellent at playing the bass at these shows and is a good friend of mine.

In 1980 Dennis and Pat George decided to move out of their Streatham home in London and move to the beautiful North Wales. Today after our third move within a short distance I still have a room at Pat's home in North Wales. Whilst there I have done all different types of work in the area ranging from window cleaner, storeman and potato roundsman, and I also worked at a vet's surgery, and in a home for people with special needs.

À gauche : sur scène au Club 100, à Londres le 24 janvier 2010.

The White Liners: Denis George (drums), Pat George (lead guitar and singing) and Brian (bass guitar)

Pat and Denis

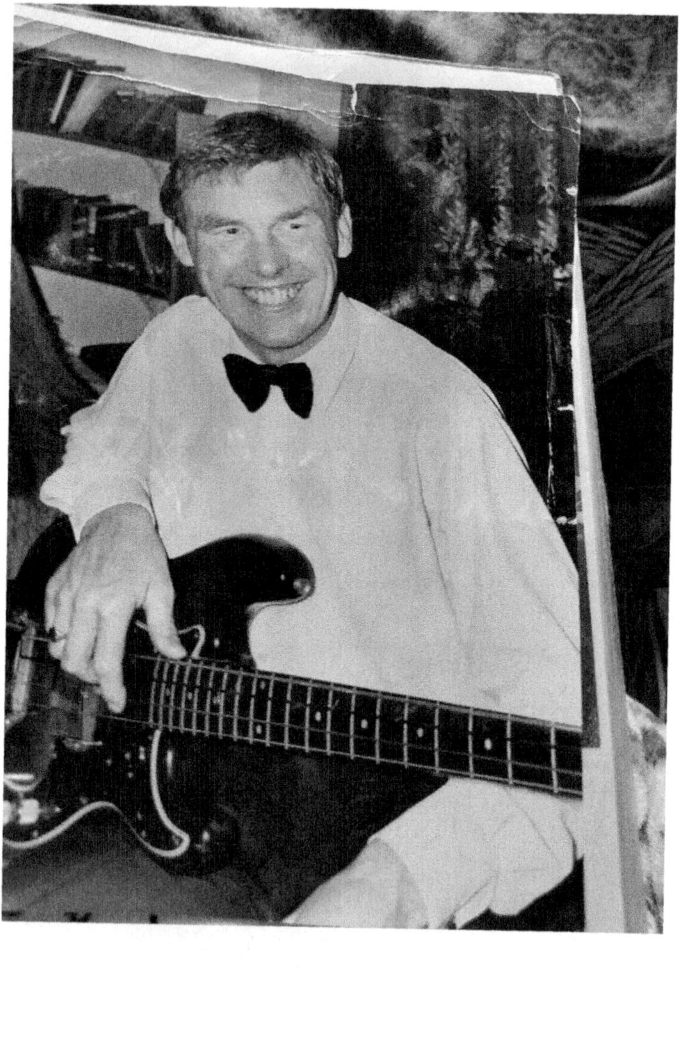

Garden in North Wales (even the cows would come and listen to Brian playing and singing!)

Tommy and Brian

RETURN TO THE MUSIC SCENE

Brian's words:

Whilst home in North Wales during 1997, I received a phone call from a John Brown, who at the time was head of the Fender Club. John asked me if I would like to become an honorary member, and I said of course I would. John informed that some of their members lived in South Wales. We contacted each other and he invited me to travel with him to the 50th anniversary trade show of Fender.

Whilst at the Fender trade show I managed to get the opportunity of playing bass on some Shadows instrumentals at Barry Gibson's Burns stand.

After the afternoon session Barry Gibson mentioned that he was putting a band together for a concert in France. The band line-up was Barry Gibson on lead guitar, Phil Kelly on rhythm, Jet Harris on bass and Clem Cattini on drums. Barry asked me if I would like to join them as part of a reunion band under the name of Local Heroes. I said yes, of course I would.

Bruce Welch also attended the French reunion and came on stage to play "Shadoogie" with us.

After the show Barry Gibson started talking to Bruce, making suggestions for a UK event remembering the music of the Shadows.

In 1998, just when I thought the idea had been forgotten about, I received a phone call from Bruce Welch. He asked me if I was interested in playing at his first *Shadowmania* event in the UK. Of course, I said yes and was happy to be working with Bruce and former musicians of the Shadows.

Apart from 1999, I had the pleasure of being invited back and appearing on stage every year Bruce organised *Shadowmania* at the Lakeside Country Club in Frimley Green, Farnham, Surrey.

Those events gave me the chance of meeting up again with Jet Harris, Tony Meehan, Bruce Welch, Brian Bennett, Alan Jones, Mark Griffiths, Warren Bennett, Cliff Hall, Mo Foster, Alan Hawkshaw, among many other musicians and friends.

Alan Jones (bass guitarist in the Shadows 1977–1989). (https://www,discogs.com)

Alan was a session bass player who started out playing lead guitar until falling under the spell of a certain Mr Jet Harris whereupon he switched to bass. Alan became part of the Johnny Howard Group which led to numerous radio appearances and then on to session. In the 1970s/80s he was one of the UK's leading session men, playing on literally thousands of session tracks including many No 1 hits. Between 1978 and 1989 Alan toured and recorded with the Shadows until a serious car accident almost ended his life. He was part of Barry Gibson's Local Heroes and part of Bruce Welsh's Bruce's Moonlight Shadows, and a regular at Pipeline and many other conventions.

Mark Griffiths
(https://en.m.wikipedia.org>wiki)

Mark is a British bassist who toured with Neil Innes in his touring ensemble of the fictional Beatles, the Rutles, where he performed Rutles songs and other songs from his career such as his songs from the Bonzo Dog Doo-Dah Band. He also played with Cliff Richard and the Shadows.

Warren Bennett (https://en.m.wikipedia.org>wiki)

Warren is an English musician, composer and performer and son of Brian Bennett, the Shadow's drummer. He has played keyboards on tour with the Shadows from 2004 until the present day. He is not only an accomplished musician, writer and producer (with over 70 albums) but also an established composer for feature films and TV shows.

Cliff Hall
(Cliff Hall The Shadows Keyboard Legend – a Facebook public group)

Cliff is a top session musician playing keyboards who has worked with the Shadows for many years, including on their final tour in 2004, Cliff Richard, Bay City Rollers, Leo Sayer, David Essex and Demis Roussos plus many more.

Mo Foster
(https://en.m.wikipedia.org>wiki)

Mo is a prestigious bass guitar player and a highly respected session musician, record producer, composer, solo artist, author and raconteur.

Alan Hawkshaw
(https://en.m.wikipedia.org>wiki)

Alan is a British composer and performer, particularly of themes for movies and television programmes. He worked in the 1960s and 1970s composing and recording many stock tracks that have been used extensively in film and TV, and also played keyboards.

Brian's words:

I am fortunate and enjoy playing my part in keeping the music of the Shadows alive. As an "ambassador" at Cliff Richard and the Shadows Clubs around the UK, I have made guest appearances at their special gala events. I have also had the pleasure of being invited overseas to Shadows Clubs in Belgium, France, Germany, Spain, Norway, Italy, Canada and the Netherlands.

It was whilst I was in the Netherlands during January/February 2004 that I teamed up with Gijs Lemmen, who I'd met previously at Joop and Jolanda Moen's Cliff Richard and the Shadows fan meeting in Tilburg. Together we worked on my first CD Licorice and Lemmen – *It's Only Natural*. In 2005 my second CD *Returning Home* was produced by the Cliff Richard and the Shadows fan club in France. Brian Bennett played on four of the tracks on this CD. My third *Harmonically Yours* was released in 2008 and gave me the opportunity to cover 14 classical numbers on my Hohner 270 chromatic harmonicas. A fourth CD, is again with Gijs Lemmen, with the Six Hand Rhythms, and is called *Swing Sweet and Smooth*.

Hank Marvin, Alan Hawkshaw, John Rostill and Brian Bennett

Kevin Harris, Biorn Arnesen, Clem Cattini, Brian, Barry Husband and Big Jim Sullivan

Brian and Bruce Welch

Brian Bennett and Brian back together again.

Cliff Hall (Shadows' keyboard player and Brian's partner in crime)

Good friends and fellow bass players: Mark Griffith, Brian and Jet Harris

REUNION

Brian's words:

On 1st May 2007, I travelled across to Halifax in West Yorkshire to see *Marty Wilde's 50th Anniversary Concert* as a member of the audience at the Victoria Theatre with some members of the East Yorkshire Shadows Guitar Club. I had not seen Marty Wilde since playing bass for him in the original Wildcats back in those late 1950s/early 60s.

The performance was excellent with Marty's two daughters, Kim and Roxanne, singing beautifully as well as a very good, polished performance from Marty and his current Wildcats.

When the concert was over, I was invited backstage to meet up with Marty again.

After recalling our past experiences Marty asked me if I would be interested in teaming up with him and playing on stage with the original Wildcats at the London Palladium on 27th May 2007 in a special concert, with other surprise guest artistes for the audience. Marty was trying to get the original Wildcats – Big Jim Sullivan, Tony Belcher, Brian Bennett and I together to perform a number on stage with him just like we used to do over 50 years ago. Was I interested? You bet I was! Of course, I was thrilled to be back on stage with Marty and the Wildcats playing my original Fender Precision bass guitar, which I had used with Marty in the late 1950s.

The number Marty selected for his original Wildcats to play was "Bad Boy" which we had recorded and released 50 years before.

Also surprise guesting at the concert was Jet Harris who played "Scarlett O'Hara", "Diamonds", and the "Theme from Something Really Important", and later in the show Hank Marvin, Bruce Welch and Brian Bennett came on stage and backed Marty on "Move It".

At the end of the show the entire cast including Hank, Bruce and Brian with Justin Hayward (the lead singer of the Moody Blues and solo singer, musician and composer in his own right, who was discovered and mentored by Marty before his career in music), Roxanne and Kim Wilde (Marty's daughters and singers in their own right), Jet Harris, and his current and original Wildcats and I all came on stage to join Marty on his final number of the night "Roll over Beethoven".

It was a wonderful experience to be back on stage with Marty and the original Wildcats of the 1950s and the Shadows 1962/3 line-up. What an evening to remember!

Babs' words:

In 2007 Dave and I were living in Skegness, Lincolnshire, and our Brian came to visit us, and he told us of how he had met up with Marty Wilde and that he had been invited to join him to be part of the show in the original Wildcats group on *Marty's Anniversary Tour* for his 50 years in showbusiness, at the London Palladium. We told him of how pleased we were for him, and then he broke the news... also appearing on the show would be Justin Hayward, the lead singer of the group The Moody Blues. WOW! That hit me like a ten-ton brick!!

The Moody Blues are only my all-time favourite band, and Justin Hayward is my all-time favourite singer idol (apart from Donovan). I immediately knew we had to try and get some tickets for the show and didn't care how much it would cost!

Brian laughed at me and said, "Oh Yes, show more interest in seeing Justin Hayward than seeing me perform in the show!" (Ha ha)!!

Of course, I wanted to see Brian perform, but the prospect of possibly actually seeing my all-time idol was awesome!!

Yes, we managed to get two tickets for me and Dave and decided that we would travel down to London via train from Grantham after stop over at our friends' house there, Bob and Sue Gardecki. (They were friends of Brian too and they knew all too well how mad I was on Justin Hayward and the Moody Blues.)

The big day came, and I was soooo excited! I decided that if by any chance I could get Brian to get me a Justin Hayward signature I would take along my Justin Hayward CD with me, and of course wear my original Moody Blues badge.

We dropped our overnight bags off at Bob and Sue's (we were returning to Grantham after the show), then caught the train to King's Cross, London. My heart was beating quite fast as I felt like it was a huge adventure.

We caught the train and started on our journey, but after few miles the train unexpectedly stopped. IT HAD BROKEN DOWN! They were unable to get it going again so all us passengers had to wait for a bus to continue our journey to London. The show was on that night, and I was terrified that we would not get there in time. The bus came and with great relief we re-started our journey again, BUT, on the motorway the bus started going slow and the driver said there was some trouble with the engine.

Oh nooooooo... we almost resigned ourselves that we would never reach London in time for the show, but after a lot of stops and starts the bus eventually got going at a fair speed again, but I felt very panicky about the time!

We finally got to King's Cross, and we dashed as fast as we could to the Underground tube train which took us to Argyle Street and the London Palladium Theatre. We practically ran there when we came out of the tube station.

Thankfully when we got there was a very large queue, but we didn't care then, we had made it... Phew!

As we were patiently waiting, we saw a figure come running out from the stage door entrance of the theatre, running toward us through the crowd of people. It was only our Brian, and he was waving some tickets in the air and shouting, "I got your tickets." I said, "But we have already got our tickets for the show." Brian said, "I know but these are your tickets for the reception party after the show." What????? And before we could properly talk to him, he said, "Gotta go now... see you later!" and he rushed back through the large crowd who by now had recognised Brian as being "one of the Shadows", and were trying to jostle him, but he managed to get back through the stage door again.

My heart was beating fast again, and it took a while to sink in that we may be allowed to go to the after-show party with the artistes in the show??? My mind was racing!

We got in the theatre, took our seats and we had a good view of the stage from the circle, and nothing was obstructing our view. Wow! It was so exciting and there were cameras around, so we knew that the show was going to be recorded.

What a fabulous show it was too, and so proud and excited to see our Brian playing on the stage and then surprised to see Jet Harris appearing too (he is so lovely), then the rest of the Shadows were there: Hank Marvin, Bruce Welch and Brian Bennett. Wow! To see them all together was amazing and loved seeing Big Jim Sullivan (our Brian's great friend and fellow Wildcat) and Brian Bennett. The atmosphere was electric and Marty Wilde was excellent.

Dave was really pleased to see his favourite lady singer performing, Kim Wilde, and her sister Roxanne (Marty's famous daughters. What a lovely, close and talented family they are), and then Justin Hayward was introduced on stage JUST WOW! I was shouting and screaming like a crazy demented teenager!!

The whole show was fantastic and we enjoyed every second of it. So, were we to meet them afterwards at the party? Surely not Justin Hayward... no, no, no,... surely, he would be having to fly back to America where he lives?

We met Brian as planned in the foyer and he took us up some stairs into a beautiful room. We felt as if we were in Buckingham Palace. Brian said he would come back shortly after he had changed. It was fantastic and everything was laid out beautifully, but I felt so nervous! We then spotted two of Brian's friends, who we had met several times before and knew quite well (from other meetings we had been to with Brian), Margaret and Diane (twin sisters), and felt more comfortable talking to them.

Other people started coming into the room and we saw Hank Marvin and his lovely wife Carole, Bruce Welch and Brian Bennett, and had photographs taken with them and they were all lovely. Then I looked across at the little bar in the room and spotted Jet Harris standing there. Feeling more confident now, I walked over to him, said hello and asked him for a pic. He immediately said, "No!" in a gruff voice, so I said (cheekily), "Aww go on, don't you know who I am?" and smiled sweetly. He smiled back and said, "Oh, alright then, seeing as its you, Brian's little sis!"

Everyone one was being really nice, then as I was talking to Dave, I heard words that nearly made me fall to the ground, "Don't look now but there is someone just walking up behind you," and at that very moment, I heard our Brian saying, "and this is my sister Barbara who I was telling you about and who is one of your biggest fans." As I turned around Justin Hayward was right in front of me, he took my hand and said, "It's a pleasure to meet you, Barbara."

Words can never describe that moment!

It just felt as if I was talking to an old friend. He was absolutely charming and so welcoming. I chatted to him ten to the dozen and we had a right good chat about him and the other band members of Moody Blues, and he was interested to hear about our experiences at their concerts and discussed some of his songs etc.

I took out my CD and he seemed impressed that I had it with me, and signed it for me, then posed for photographs. Just Wow!!

I found out later that our Brian had shared the dressing room with him, and he had spoken to him at length about me.

My favourite song of all time is "Nights in White Satin", and Brian said he wished he had the opportunity to accompany Justin on this song with his harmonica.

Brian would always play this just for me whenever we were together.

After Justin had left, I looked over and Dave was in deep conversation with Kim Wilde, and they were having a great conversation, and sharing laughs and jokes together!

Brian then took us over to meet Marty Wilde and some more of his musical friends, including a really lovely lady who had been one of the Vernon Girls in the 50s TV show *Oh Boy*.

The whole party was going with a lovely swing, and everyone was so friendly. The only thing that spoilt it was that we had to leave to catch the tube train, then the train back to Grantham. How I wished we had arranged to stay the night somewhere in London, but what a fabulous time we had had!!

On the way home we just couldn't stop talking about it, and poor Bob and Sue when we returned to their house, they had to listen to the whole story and none of us got much sleep that night. I often watch that show now on YouTube and re-live that night. Thank you, our Brian. XX

BORN TO ROCK N' ROLL

MARTY WILDE

IN CONCERT
50TH ANNIVERSARY TOUR
With THE WILDCATS
and special guests

SOUVENIR PROGRAMME
www.flyingmusic.com

Original Wildcats with Marty Wilde, Brian (bass), Brian Bennett (drums) and Big Jim Sullivan (lead guitar)

Marty and Justin, and our super-duper meeting with Justin.

MUSICAL VENUES WITH FRIENDS AND FELLOW MUSICIANS

Brian's words:

On 5th February 2011, the man I had replaced in the Shadows, Jet Harris, gave what was to be his last public performance. It took place at the Ferneham Hall, Fareham in Surrey. Jet was playing guitar, I joined him on harmonica and Alan Jones on bass guitar – three former Shadows' bass players all on stage at the same time.

Six weeks later, after a long illness, Jet sadly passed away on 18th March 2011

The wonderful Jet Harris. Such a dear friend of Brian's.

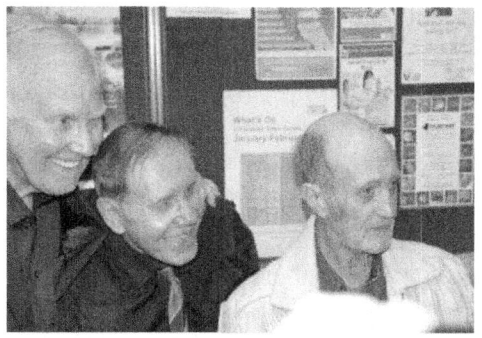

Last days and performance with Jet, Alan Jones and Brian.

SHADOWMANIA

Bruce Welch's Shadows:

In 1998 Bruce Welch of the Shadows arranged his iconic *Shadowmania* event at the Lakeside Country Club Frimley, in Surrey which continued annually until 2012. *Shadowmania* was a get-together for "Shadow-Maniacs" everywhere and many travelled from all over the world just to be there.

Every year the programme comprised of guitar instrumental groups from the UK and abroad, and guests associated with the Shadows, such as Jet Harris, Brian "Licorice" Locking, Alan Jones, Warren Bennett and Cliff Hall, and many others.

Record Collector **(issue 382)**

Review of *Shadowmania*, Lakeside Country Club, 18th September 2010 by Melvyn Dover

Bruce Welch remembered loyal *Shadowmania* fans and Shadows old and new joined Shadows-soundalike bands to celebrate their music.

Switzerland's Indra and Move it backed "Licorice" Locking, the shortest-serving bassist with the Shadows. He still plays a mean bass and sang in French, before switching to harmonica. "My Prayer" received a standing ovation.

The Shadowers, who have the best lookalike lead guitarist Justin Daish, backed Shadows' bassist Jet Harris, who lit up on stage, briefly. All part of the act, which included his most famous hit, "Diamonds".

Welch then took to the stage with his Shadows' bass stalwart, Alan Jones, as solid as a rock, and partnered by keyboardist Cliff Hall brought a sense of fun on stage. Bob Watkins on drums and Phil Kelly on lead completed the line-up as they performed hits and rarities in a two-hour spot. It ended with high kicking along to "F.B.I."

Brian "Licorice" Locking Facebook private group site – Kev Moore

In the late 90s, Brian became a regular at Bruce Welch's *Shadowmania* fan gatherings at The Lakeside Country Club, Surrey, and was always a popular guest at Shadows-related fan meetings throughout Europe, where his willingness to sit in bands, play bass and harmonica and chat about his career made him a popular and much-loved guest. Brian was also a regular visitor to Canada.

He visited in 2000/2001 when a group was started for Shadows' fans/musicians by Roger Lapworth, that then led to the formation of the Toronto Shadows Club. Brian played at some famous Toronto venues. The Silver Dollar was one, with Danny Marks. He also played at *Shadowmania North America* on at least three occasions including 2006. He played at many other venues around the Toronto area, and on occasions Brian's good friend Pat would attend.

PRESENTS
SHADOWMANIA
1958
2000
To Dave & Barbara

PRESENTS
SHADOWMANIA
SATURDAY 30TH MAY
3.00 PM-LATE
LAKESIDE COMPLEX
WHARF ROAD, FRIMLEY GREEN,
LIVE ON STAGE
BRUCE WELCH'S
MOONLIGHT
SHADOWS
JET HARRIS
'LICORICE' LOCKING
FBI
THE RAPIERS
THE YOUNG ONES GUITARIST COMPETITION
DEMONSTRATION ROOM
A CELEBRATION OF
40
FABULOUS YEARS
OF SHADOWS MUSIC

Bruce Welch and Brian

The "high kicking" Rapiers (Shadows tribute and instrumental band)

Jimmy Jermaine (Cliff Richard tribute) and the 7abulous Shadows

The wonderful Footappers

Great show from Peter Donegan (son of Lonnie Donegan). His first time at *Shadowmania* and introduced by Brian. He was just amazing as well as all the acts appearing there.

Me and "sis" Gill Pugh showing off our Shadows moves.

Very special moment watching the lovely Jet Harris performing on stage.

2I'S COFFEE BAR, OLD COMPTON STREET, SOHO, LONDON

Brian's words:

Each year I am invited to take part in the *2i's Coffee Bar Reunion Day* at the 100 Club in London's Oxford Street.

We all meet up with Vince Eager, Clem Cattini, Wee Willie Harris, Chas McDevitt, Terry Dene and many of the original artistes who started their musical careers in the 2i's Coffee Bar (also other younger musician friends would get involved, including Brian's friends, Kevin Harris and Barry Husband).

Back in 1957 in the height of the coffee bar era, the music was frantic and had that raw amateur feel about it. Rock 'n' Roll was played with the minimum amount of equipment and unlike today where technology has advanced to the extent where you could recreate a studio sound on a stage with professionally arranged music. Back in those early days of Rock 'n' Roll it was the raw sound that created such a great atmosphere down in the basement of the 2i's Coffee Bar.

Today the 2i's has been converted into an Italian restaurant and the basement where I used to perform would not be acceptable today because of stricter health and safety regulations.

The small stage (planks of wood on milk crates) that used to be in the corner is now the restaurant's toilets. There were no toilets in the 2i's; you would have had to walk round to Leicester Square (probably about a mile away!).

For years people had been trying to get the building recognised as being the birthplace of rock 'n' roll in Britain.

On 18th September 2006, Westminster council, with pressure from my friend Robert Mandry, decided to erect a green plaque on the site of the 2i's Coffee Bar.

I was fortunate to be invited along with Cliff Richard, Bruce Welch and Brian Bennett from the Shadows, Tony Belcher and Big Jim Sullivan from the the Wildcats, Wee Willie Harris, Chas McDevitt, Russ Sainty, Vince Eager, John D'Avensac, Tex Makins, Clem Cattini, Rick Hardy, Barry Woodman, John Allison, and many other rock 'n' roll performers who started their careers at the 2i's to the unveiling ceremony of this long overdue green plaque on this famous building in London's Old Compton Street.

The 2i's was part of the rock 'n' roll legacy and holds many happy memories for me. It was of course a huge part of my musical life in the late 1950s and early 1960s.

Working with top musicians and vocalists of that period was a turning point in my life and gave me the opportunity to build up my experience by working with such a variety of artistes, who all had their individual styles of performing.

Babs' words:

Whilst I was reading through some of Brian's writings and memorabilia, I came across a handwritten poem written by a Gerry Champion on 18th September 2006, with a signature on it from Cliff Richard.

This appears as great tribute to this famous coffee bar and appropriate to end this chapter of history.

THE TWO EYES LEGEND

Paul Lincoln and Tom Littlewood soon to be renowned

Decided to run a coffee bar, which was soon to rock Soho Town,

From 1956 when Tommy Steele was grooving,

The Two Eyes was the joint to get you really movin',

From miles around musicians came both instrumental and vocal,

Entertaining those who packed in each night, both sightseers and local,

The Vipers were the favourites with their own brand of skiffle,

Their followers one and all agreed and other music's "piffle",

Then USA's Haley and Elvis, Gene, Jerry and Eddie, Richard, Buddy and the Big Bopper,

Soon changed the scene to rock 'n' roll, and skiffle became a cropper.

The Two Eyes welcomed one and ALL to come and show their talent, new names in idols topped the bill, names all true rockers knew,

Wee Willie Harris, Terry Dene, Marty Wilde, Danny Rivers too, Cliff Richard, Rory Blackuet, Vince Eager, Vince Taylor, Keith Kelly, to name but a few,

Not forgetting the Great Dave "Lord Sutch",
and his Roving Savages too.
Many more graced Two Eyes' stage, some good in between,
Was this to be their rise to Fame? Or just a Teenage Dream?
As the Two Eyes alas has passed and all that's left is the Ghost,
Of times when rock 'n' roll was king, and the Two Eyes was its host.

Gerry Champion

2 I's Coffee Bar – Chas. Vince Taylor and Tony Sheridan

Back to the 2i's

It may well be a bar / restaurant now, but 59 Old Compton Street in London's Soho district was once home to the famed 2i's coffee bar from which many a career was launched back in the late '50s. On September 18th, several of those British artists with a connection to the 2i's returned to witness the unveiling of one of the City of Westminster's Green Plaques acknowledging that the 2i's was the "Birthplace of British rock n roll and the popular music industry".

All photos © John D'Avensac and Chas McDevitt

The Vagabonds
2i's Coffee Bar 1957

The Vagabonds
Grantham 2015

THE 2-I's COFFEE CLUB
59, Old Compton Street, London, W.1

MEMBER'S CARD

This is to certify that

is a Member of the above Club

The Wildcats/Krew kats (Tony Belcher, Brian, Brian Bennett and Big Jim SULLIVAN)

GREAT 2i's rockers at the birth of rock 'n' roll. THANK YOU ALL FOR YOUR MUSIC.
XXXXXXXXXXXXXXXXXXXXXXXXXXXXXXXXXXXXXX
XXXXXXXXXXXXXX

TRIBUTES

Personal message from Eduardo Bartrina, Los Jets group, Madrid, Spain"

Los Jets have been Spain's premier rock instrumental band for over 40 years. Albums including *Spanish Blood*, *40 Aniversario* and *The Essential*. They have fans all over the world with their unique and enticing brand of guitar music. (DWM music company)

Eduardo Bartrina de Caso was the band's drummer until the day of the *Final Concert* on 31st October 2009.

Eduardo is now a successful novelist who has written a tribute book to Brian and Bruce Welch and several mysterious fiction books.

From my youth I knew who Brian Locking was through the album folders of the Shadows, until in 2004 I met him personally in Holland. There he was invited to the *Tilburg Festival*, where my band Los Jets, were also part of the show.

I shook his hand, I gave him a Los Jets album, which had been the album of the year in *Pipeline* magazine. I took a photo with him, which I still have, and all that was the beginning of a great friendship.

Since then, we have been in countless festivals throughout Europe, until the idea of recording an album came up with him and I, by hand in my recording studio. To do this, he travelled to Spain to spend part of the summer holidays that year, and since then he has returned on many occasions to my house on the outskirts of Madrid, to bathe in the pool, to walk in the garden stroking my dogs, to play with my grandchildren making magic with a handkerchief, and to share with my friends, parties and wines, being admitted as someone of my family.

We recorded two more albums during his visits, and he was even our guest star at the Los Jets concerts in Spain, including my band's *Farewell Concert* in 2009 and one at the Zaragoza Expo.

But what I remember with more affection and pleasure was when after dinner we sat on the porch of the garden of my pool chatting quietly, having a good glass of wine, whilst we refreshed ourselves with the soft wind that blew after a hot day of August.

We talked about a thousand things, not just about music, and that's how I realised that Brian "Licorice" Locking,

"Lic" for the intimate ones, was an educated person, endearing, and a perfect gentleman, but above all he was my friend, someone I will never forget and will always be proud to have known, not because he was the bassist for the Shadows, just because we were friends.

Brian, Eduardo and Pat George

Eduardo's specially written tribute book to Brian, and Bruce Welch and his association with them as a fellow musician and friend.

Los Jets *50th Anniversary Concert*

Martin "Nightbird" Nachtweyh

Message to Brian:

A Hohner-Chromatic harmonica with 16 holes and the beginning of a special friendship

The very first time I met Brian was in September 1997 in Eindhoven, the Netherlands in May 1998; we met again at Bruce Welch's *Shadowmania* at Lakeside.

Before the beginning of the show, I proudly showed Brian my 16-hole Hohner chromatic harmonica – The Larry Adler Professional 16. I was pretty surprised when Brian suddenly took the harmonica out of my hand and played a few bars on it. Nobody but Brian would have done so. He was highly impressed by the warm sound of this instrument. (I think he only knew this model from Hohner catalogues, because he preferred a small-sized one on stage.) Then Brian tested my humour and asked me, with a wide grin on his face: "May I keep it?" My answer was: "Yes, but you have to pay for it." After that we both had to laugh out loud. This was the beginning of a special friendship.

"Dakota" and more – The Day I Met Brian (For the First Time)

Ode to my dear late friend Brian
By Martin "Nightbird" Nachtweyh

My poem begins in the Netherlands.
I was among the two hundred fans
Which had been coming to attend
A Shad's fan meeting, an event
Well-organised by some Dutch friends.
The show was shared by four cover bands.
I still well remember that great event.
I travelled together with a friend
In his old car – without a dame.
Eindhoven was the Dutch town's name.
And we were full of expectation
When reaching our destination.

Our table neighbours in a motel's hall
Were two Dutch ladies, pretty and tall.
We enjoyed the Dutch club's show
Nearly twenty-four years ago.
And for the first time in my life
I saw my harmonica idol live.
I was delighted to see Brian there: this great musician with light grey hair
and the radiant smile on his face,
playing harmonica and on bass.
The LOCAL HEROES backed him on stage.
(By the way, I was then fifty of age.)
Their performance was simply excellent
And one of the highlights of the event.

Another hero was backed by this band
originating in Shadowland:
Jet Harris, bass player of the SHADS
When Hank & Co were still young lads.

But back to the title of my rhyme.
"The Day I Met Brian (For the First Time)":
I was proud of his autograph on an EP
In the year two thousand minus three,
On the twenty-seventh of September,
A Saturday I still clearly remember.

****

When I hold my harmonica in my hand,
I must think of Brian, my dear late friend,
A great musician and a gentleman.
(Whose duo partner I was now and then
In Germany, Denmark and Switzerland).
Now Living in Peace in a Wonderful Land.

Personal message:

Swisshad Shadows group (Switzerland), a tribute:

In 2012 the Swisshad Shadows fan group had a special meeting on 16th June in Switzerland where Brian was invited and attended as a special guest. He was warmly welcomed by all members and participated in musical performances alongside the Joeland Plus guitar sound group. Members being Roland Sigried (lead, rhythm and bass), Joel Siefried (lead rhythm and bass), Roger Hayoz (lead, rhythm bass) and Ulle Bayer (drums).

Also, Brian was presented with a unique and exclusive present, especially put together for Brian as gratitude for his participation at the meeting. This was a book of dates and pictures out of a private collection created by Heinz M. Rolli (chronikman-ch) from Switzerland and presented to Brian by Heinz.

***Swisshad* tribute by Ulle Bayer**

Swisshad Remembers 2012 And 2013

Our friend Brian Locking at

***Swisshad 2012*, Bosingen, Switzerland:**
It is the first time in 40 years that an original member of the Shadows in Switzerland is actively on a stage, and this is due to him and the visitors of the event.

Since 2006 Brian and I are now friends and often share stage and private things with each other. Together with my musicians from Joeland Plus we are planning a Shadows tribute event in Switzerland and Brian is thankfully ready to come and support us musically.

We appreciate Brian's willingness to succeed on our occasions and have prepared some surprises to thank him.

He enthusiastically tells me that he would have like to be greeted at the airport on every occasion. One of our young female members of Joeland Guitar Sound, Sandra, picked him up in Kioten.

In 2012, Brian was very touched by the fact that probably the biggest Shadows' fan in Switzerland, Heinz Rolli from Bern, wrote a 1000-page book, *The Shadows Day by Day – Facts 1958–2004*, and wrote a "Special version" for Brian and presented this book to him on stage as a gift.

In 2013 we invited one of his greatest friends, Martin Natchweych, and his wife Karen to the event. Both arrived from near Hamburg. Brian and Martin knew each other very well, as they have repeatedly performed together as a harmonica duo and Brian lived with them at various events in Bad Oldesloe. Of course, the two also performed together musically.

The biggest surprise for Brian, however, was that I met his former girlfriend, who lives near Zurich, and invited her to Bosingen. They met in London and met again for the first time at Swisshad 2013 after more than 50 years of separation.

After the events we enjoyed many hours together wherever we performed together. In addition to basic musical training –Brian was a brilliant music teacher for me – the humour was never neglected. On one occasion Brian told me that he had once even worked as a fireman on a steam locomotive after school – but his career was quickly over, after he threw the shovel into the fire at the first throw in addition to the coals. We kept laughing about it!

We also laughed at dinner together with Karen and Martin Natchweych, as well as my wife Antoinette. Brian probably did not trust the proposed Swiss specialities and ordered fish. However, he was fascinated by my wife Antoinette's food, and he asked if he could try some of it. Finally, my wife ate the fish and he ate the legendary Swiss dish "Zurich Geschnetites Mit Roschti".

Brian mentioned, "This was one of my most beautiful in my life... all that is missing is the plum cake." I was prepared for this, and his wish was fulfilled at the late hour.

For Brian:

Brian – we have performed with you almost all over Europe and you have always supported us with your expertise, music and humour. When I think about it, you are the only Shadow who has lived this music for many long years with your commitment. You are incredible, dear gentleman. I will never forget you.

Ulle

19TH SHADOWS MUSIC CONVENTION
7TH OCTOBER 2017
live in concert:
Tasty (N)
Jumping Jewels Revival Band (NL)
Marvin's Erben
De Schädoos (D)
im
"Niedersachsenhof" Haag's Hotel
Lindhooper Strasse 97
27283 Verden (Aller), Germany
Tel: 0 4231 66 60 Fax: 0 4231 6 48 75
Beginn: 14:00 h
Open end
Horst Schröder, Postfach 245, 24206 Preetz
Tel.: 0 4142 8 65 05 (AB)
Horst Schröder

THE SHADOWS KNOW!!!
SHINDIG
ATLANTIS

Roland Siegfried

Guitarist, founder Joeland Plus and CEO Swiss Shadows community:

My first meeting with Brian was on 22nd May 2010 at the *19th Shadows Convention* in Rimini, Italy. We played there with Joeland Plus. For my son Joel and for me it was the first time to be so close to a real legend. Our drummer Ulle Bayer, on the other hand, had known Brian for many years from various events like Lakeside etc. At that time, I was 54 years old and had been playing the Shadows numbers for over 40 years in various formations. All the greater was the joy and pride, but also the awe to suddenly stand in front of such a famous rock pioneer and even play music together with him on stage.

The nervousness quickly vanished, Brian knew how to captivate us with his inimitable charm, friendliness and empathy. It was the beginning of a wonderful friendship over all the years to come.

Joel was 14 years old at the time and naturally attracted a lot of attention thanks to his age, as there was an age difference of 50 years from the youngest to the oldest of us.

Brian once said to me that I was already a very good guitarist, but Joel was exceptional. That made me very happy and proud. Brian and Joel got on very well together.

In the following years we played together with Brian on stage several times, be it in Germany, Holland or Switzerland. There were also private contacts.

For concerts in Germany, he was usually looked after by Martin Nachtweyht. I remember well that we, that is Martin, Ulle and I, picked Brian up at the airport in Hamburg in the evening and drove from there directly to the Shadows event in Verden. For this several-hour drive, Martin had always prepared a snack for Brian, which consisted of tea, two sandwiches and 1lb of plums. This was already a tradition and Brian always looked forward to those plums!

On one Friday morning, Martin picked up Ulle and me, and this is an unforgettable story. Martin had a spare car, as his was in the workshop. There are three huge car park towers at Hamburg airport. Now our dear Martin no longer knew in which tower he had parked the car, and neither could he remember the model of the car, so we had to search for over two hours until we finally found it, and poor Martin was close to a nervous breakdown!!

Brian always stayed overnight at Karen and Martin Nachtweyht's and we spent may convivial hours together. Once Brian tried to teach me the "Shadows Walk", but I couldn't pull off the nonchalance and elegance, and as a result I didn't do it.

In July 2013, Joel and I were asked by Eduardo Bartrina, drummer of the legendary Los Jets from Spain, to record a CD with him and Brian. It was a great honour, and with much joy we flew to Madrid to spend a wonderful week in Eduardo's studio. The studio was air-conditioned to a lovely 19 degrees, whilst outside it was 40 degrees. The CD *Where were we* as Three Amigos was released in the year 2013 and was voted album of the year 2013 in various trade magazines.

Further meetings in the following years also took place outside our concerts. I still remember well that we surprised Brian in Duisburg at the *Guitar Heroes of the World* event. Brian was there as a special guest in the programme and played a few tracks with the Spotnicks, among others. However, he felt somehow lost and was so happy to see us that he almost cuddled us to death!

After he had retired a bit from big travelling in the last few years, we intended to visit him in England. Unfortunately Covid-19 threw a spanner in the works, and with Brian's passing in October 2020, there was no chance of that happening.

However, Brian will always be remembered by us as a wonderful person, musician and gentleman. It has been an honour to count Brian among our friends all these years.

I close my report with Brian's words in German:

BITTE SCHON – DANKE SCHON – GERN GESCHELHEN.

Roland

Joeland with Brian 'Licorice' Locking

Arild Brekken (Norway)

A story of Brian:

There is the fact that Brian was very fond of having lots of reverb on his harmonica when it went through the PA system. I can't remember where it was, but at a soundcheck once where we were also booked to play with the Reflections, Brian kept asking for more and more reverb, as he almost always did. After asking several times for more, the sound guy replied, slightly irritated, "You've got it all already mate, there's no reverb left, even for the other bands!" I thought that was rather funny!

We all remember Brian as a very nice and friendly person, a true gentleman and a fine musician.

His magic tricks were neat as well. He was always smiling, joking and in a good mood which affected everybody in the room. Such a friendly way of dealing with everybody, like fans that wanted his picture or autograph etc. Seeing him again always meant a big warm hug that literally took your breath away.

Together with my bandmates, I have had the great honour of knowing Brian for several years from the late 90s, and performing with him on stage on numerous occasions in various countries during the years. There are so many great memories, that I wouldn't even know how to start.

On behalf of my colleagues in the two bands, the Reflections and the Internationals, we are all very sorry for your loss and send our love and condolences to you and his family.

Brian will be missed greatly and will always have a special place in our hearts.

With warm thoughts and love.
Svein A. Tjemsland, Kjetil Brekken, Ole R. Gudmestad, Arild Brekken (The Reflections)

Martin De Lefde, Maalte Weber, Andreas Leber, Arild Brekken (The Internationals)

Arild Brekken (Norway) and Brian

Jeroen de Vries:

I was born when the Shads were about to split up, but it hasn't stopped me at all being a huge fan of their wonderful tunes. In 1983 I heard a Shadows tune first time and I was sold. A year later I started guitar course (classical) and my present for graduation at high school was of course an electric guitar. I kept on playing Shadows and other 60s music and joined my group Gee Whizz in 1993.

In 1989 I started visiting the Shadows meetings in the Netherlands, and for years I was the youngest attendant, just 19 or 20 years old. I remember some visitors asking me if I'd entered the wrong building! But no one could keep me away!!

After 32 years they know me now, as I have played in the demo room and on the main stage with the Gee Whizz band.

In 2001 I met Brian for the first time during the jubilee version of the *40th International Fan Meeting* in Berkel-Enschot. The organiser, Joop Moen, arranged a surprise by asking Brian to play "Lucky Lips" with us, and it was a very pleasant experience to have a real "Shadows" bass player joining us on the stage, but the real story starts here.

In approx. 2005 I did my usual hanging around in the demo area at the *Cliff and Shadows Fan Meeting* in Berkel-Enschot. I did not play as I was too shy to play when there was a big crowd of people.

The crew, who I had known for years and who owned the Fenders and VOC-amps, asked me if I could watch over the Jam-room, as they were going for dinner in the restaurant, Druiventros.

They allowed me to use the equipment and so I started playing, and very soon two other guests from the meeting joined me playing rhythm guitar and drums.

We played about two or three Shadows tunes, and a few people watched from the doorstep but soon left, as playing without a bass guitar sounded a bit empty. Then Brian came into the room, walked right up to the stage, grabbed the available precision bass, and gave us a sign to start the song again from the beginning.

This we did and we had a fantastic "jam" of four Shadows songs. I didn't have time to get nervous or star-struck as halfway through the second song "Peace Pipe", I looked over my glasses and noticed the room was packed with people beyond the doorstep!

Having played with Brian was an experience I cherish to this day, and in following years we met more often and played "Sleepwalk" and other numbers together.

The last time we met, he was extremely thankful when I gave him a few mini discs so he could prepare some harmonica backing tracks.

He will be sorely missed at all Shadows meetings globally. Brian was great and I'm more than happy to have these memories and his signature on my precious 1979 Fender Stratocaster.

Still miss ya my friend!

Brian "Licorice" Locking Facebook sites

Babs' words:

Brian has never owned a computer and has not shown an interest in using social media as he has always preferred to talk to people and his friends and family privately, although he was provided with a small computer by his local Jehovah Witness Church, so as he could communicate with them during the Covid-19 lockdown period, but he did have difficulties understanding computer technology, with the extra pressures of his failing eyesight and deteriorating health.

He was able to, at times, be shown by others his personal social media website dedicated to him, and messages sent to him, and when we were with him, we would read them out to him.

The above sites are run very efficiently by Kev Moore, Mark Cunningham, Susan Thompson, Paul Maidment, and Brian's is included in many other Cliff Richard and Shadows sites. It is wonderful to share news, pictures, videos and communications with each other, and we have loved to read them (and are still reading them!), as we know Brian was very touched by them also.

I have taken a few comments from them, but so sorry I can't include them all in this book, but they have been read and truly appreciated, and thanks to everyone for support and love shown to Brian and us. Xx

Cliff Richard (personal message):

I am really saddened by the loss of Brian "Licorice" Locking. He was one of us, in the Shadows for many years and we will miss him.

He was special for me as he is the one who first put my feet onto my Spiritual Path.

Thanks Brian... I'll always be grateful.

God bless and Rest in Peace... Cliff

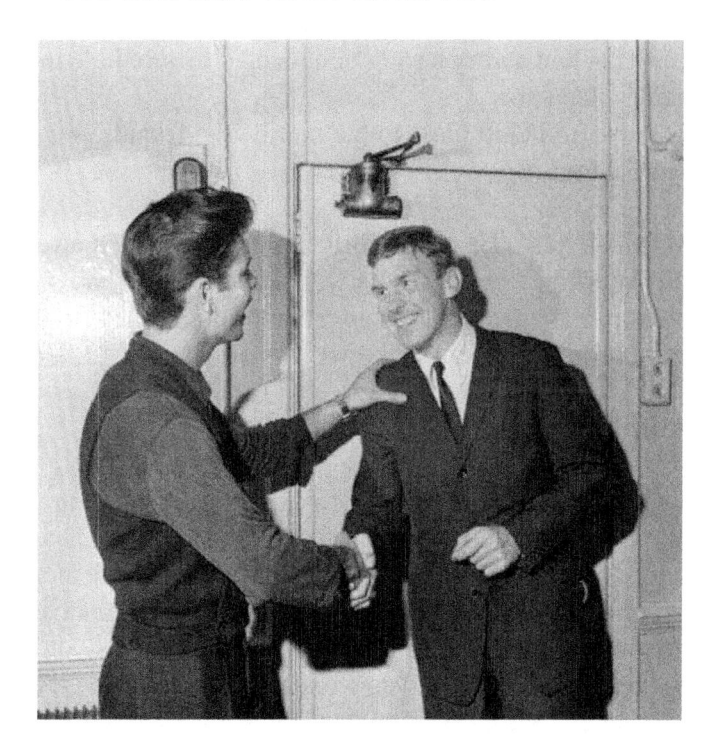

Mark Cunningham:

Very sad to hear that Shadows legend and our friend Brian has passed.

Seems every couple of days we hear of some of our favourite legends have passed.

And always sad to write RIP next to their names.

With Brian it is different and an extra sadness because I got a chance to meet him and share a stage with him.

He was a genuine nice man and he'll never know how amazing it was for me to be up there rocking with him.

Brian had a very strong belief and I'm sure he's in a better place now.

Love and God bless to his family and friends.

June Clayton:

Very sad news Brian "Licorice" Locking passed away this morning. Such a lovely, lovely man; I had the pleasure of meeting him in Scarborough. RIP Brian, another of life's gentlemen we've lost xx

Ashley Walker:

The first time we met Brian Locking, he was telling us all how he started with entertainment, who he played music with, and so forth, he helped young and more experienced bass guitar players and one time he played the harmonica. Brian played it beautifully, you could not hear a pin drop, it was wonderful.

I asked that time if he would make a CD recording which he did and he kept on playing his harmonica as well. I asked Brian to get Hank over from Perth, Australia; he must have done a lot of praying as we did too, so it's been so wonderful to meet Brian and the gifts he and they shared with us all his time, his personality and love for people. Thank you.

Please rest in peace Brian and lots of hugs to his family and friends worldwide.

Ashley and Christine

Phill Surr:

First met Brian in 1975 when we moved to Denbigh, North Wales. I was 14, now 59, he was in the local congregation. He became good friends with my dad. My dad played keyboards. They are now both in God's memory awaiting the resurrection. He had very strong belief, as did my father. I sincerely hope it is all true for you both. Best wishes to his family and all who were privileged to know him.

Roderick John Cronin:

Good night, Brian. I will miss not catching up with you. Thank you for being the gentleman that you were here on earth which means that catching up will have to wait until our spirits collide.

Debbie Anna Marie Ford:
(pics /videos and music sent)

Here is a special tribute from my hubby, looking back on some of Brian's career.

I used to show this video on a big screen for the audience when Brian came to play with me in West Yorkshire. I had such a wonderful time filled with lots of fun and laughter.

Brian' favourite to play with me was "Sleepwalk", and it was his bass that made that tune so special because he played something different every time we played it together which used to throw a surprise in the mix. We used to look at each other and he would give a little cheeky grin. I will miss our times together Brian and cherish them for as long as I live.

All my Shadows live performances are, and always will be, dedicated to you mate. You are a musical legend, a true gentleman and friend.

Georges De Palo:

Really still a friendly bass player who will join the light.

Shadows in French is shadow... he will have been very bright anyway by his presence in our favourite group!! RIP
BRIAN LICORICE.

Memories from the past by Brian Bennett (BB) (by kind agreement from BB):

In the summer of 1961 Alan Hawkshaw was playing piano on one of the seaside piers in Great Yarmouth with Emile Ford and the Checkmates. Someone in the show had told him there was a drummer he should check out playing in the pit of the Windmill Theatre.

So, one afternoon during a matinee he turned up to see who this drummer was and introduced himself. They talked about their love of jazz and immediately started to jam on some of the standard jazz repertoire.

Alan was influenced by Oscar Peterson and the drummer was a big Shelly Manne fan. For the rest of that summer season, they would meet every night after the show at The Savoy Hotel restaurant and with Brian Locking on bass, Alan Randall on vibes and occasionally Bruce Forsythe on piano, jam until the early hours. The pit drummer was me and we have been the very best of friends for over 60 years.

Martin Verrill (drummer with Legend – Shadows tribute band):

Legend had the great pleasure and privilege of playing alongside "Lic" many times. We had a load of laughs and played some great music. One of our popular *Lunchtime with Legend* was around the summer of 2004 in the café of Whitby's Spa Pavilion.

John Evans:

Quite a few memories of times we had.
http://johnevansmusic.co.uk/brian-liquorice-locking-stewart-jones-live
JOHNEVANSMUSIC.CO.UK

Personal message:

A personal tribute from very close and dear friends of Brian and who helped our Brian so extremely well in his latter days (of which we are extremely grateful for).
Thank you David and Anne Sylvester.
(Babs and Dave xx)

Brian had been telling me how he went to Europe from time to time and met up with various Shadows tribute acts – to the delight of the many Shadows' fans.

This one particular gathering was in April 2019, near St Etienne in France. It would have a double meaning for me; one I would be able to see Brian perform in a professional environment, and secondly, it would give me an excuse to visit a part of France that is very dear to me, as I first went there when I was at school. As it transpired it gave me a third reason to meet up with two French friends from those schooldays.

Brian talked to me about the upcoming evert, when he would be performing with Guitar Express (the Shadows tribute group), and with Ricky Norton, the lead singer.

I didn't let on, but my wife and I made plans to travel to the venue, to surprise Brian. Ferries and overnight accommodation were booked, tickets for the show were reserved.

We arrived the day before to pick up our tickets from the local town hall. The ladies behind the reception desk thought it was wonderful that we had motored all that way to surprise our friend and support their local event.

That evening Anne and I went to the venue to ensure we knew where it was, and there would be no problems the next evening. We learned that there was to be a reception for Brian and the band prior to the performance in a local restaurant. We located that location. Finally, we met up with my French friend and his wife, who would be attending the concert.

Jumping forward to the afternoon of the performance, we gate crashed the reception, largely with the help of my French friend!

In we went and patiently waited for Brian and his entourage to arrive. At the appropriate time, we took the opportunity to spring our surprise on Brian. I think the expression is "Gob Smacked!". He had a big smile on his face and flung his arms around us. What a moment!!

Off to the performance. It was in a large sports hall that gradually filled to capacity. I was taken aback to see so many people there all eagerly anticipating the show.

Guitar Express kicked off the show and at a pre-arranged time in the performance, the Guitar Express bass player retired from the scene and the "Big Man" took over. The crowd were enthralled by Brian's appearance and the music being played. What a memorable musical act.

We met Brian after the show for one more little chat. He obviously had to look after his many adoring fans.

We returned home and at some point, Brian and I talked about the experience. I told him he was a born actor and that he came alive when he was up there on the stage.

From time to time Brian would visit us for afternoon tea or a meal. The time would come for us to sit down in the lounge and talk about this and that. Inevitably there would be some reminiscing about his time with the Shadows.

I remember on one occasion finding clips on YouTube from the film *Summer Holiday*. I'm sure it gave Brian to re-live those times. Because not only did we see his acting capabilities, but we also talked about being the scenes events, filming location, accommodation, food, meeting up with other famous people.

How the other half live!!!

In late 2010 we didn't know how poorly Brian was. Life was obviously difficult for him, and he did his best to soldier on.

After one of our trips to the hospital Brian mentioned that he would love a McDonald's. Making a short detour to the drive-through and then on to Colwyn Bay, we parked up on the esplanade.

Brian devoured the burger and coffee and clearly thoroughly enjoying it. We sat there for a short while longer, enjoying the breaking waves and sharing our thoughts.

The simple things in life!

Personal message:

Colin Pryce-Jones (lead guitarist of the Rapiers and close friend of Brian)

"Licorice" was appearing at a Shadows festival in Holland and the Rapiers were also on the bill. We always had great times together at events.

At this Dutch event, he recounted his "Chicken Walk" story (if you saw "Licorice" with the Rapiers at the 2015 Lakeside Shadows day playing "Dakota", you may have wondered why I introduced him as loving to do the "Chicken Walk", which he did as he came on the stage).

This certain Shadows day was taking place in a large room at an event complex, opposite us was another room full of people. "Licorice" said that they all looked a might miserable, so to cheer them up, thinking they were part of the Shadows convention, he entered the room and did a complete circle of the seated people doing the "Chicken Walk" with his trademark smile.

Feeling pleased with himself he was surprised to see a stern gentleman walking toward him, asking why he was doing this AT A FUNERAL!!!!!

"Licorice" became such a good friend to me, and I am so grateful to have known him. We spent many hours on the telephone when we were not together at gigs. "Licorice" was there at the very beginning of the British rock 'n' roll story and had always kept his love of those wonderful times. His harmonica playing was exemplary.

THANK YOU "Licorice" for the music and for being such a real gentleman and friend to us all.

GOD BLESS YOU ALWAYS XXXXXX

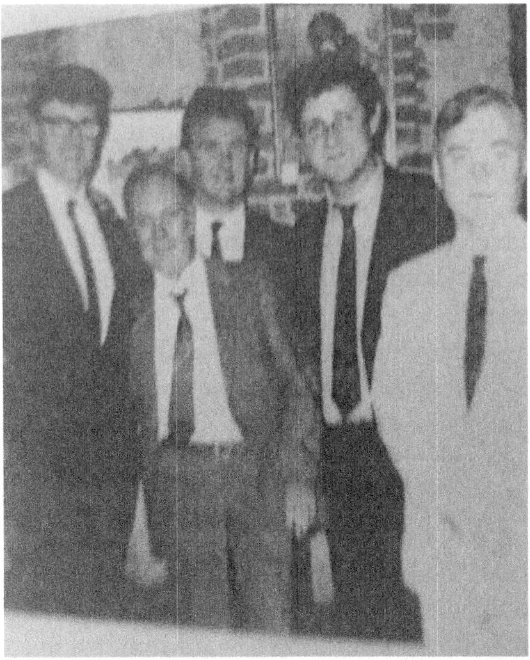

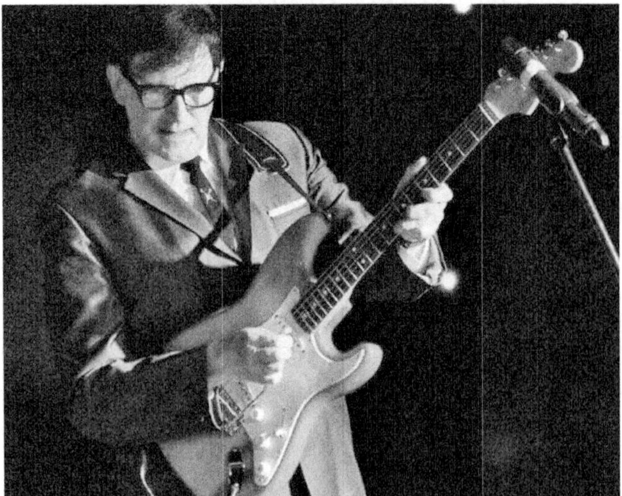

Personal reminisce from a friend
June Pulfrey

Babs' words:

I remember June, who lived just around the corner from our family in Grantham, but I never knew her, only recognised her face, and she only recently contacted me when she heard about Brian's illness and of course his passing, and she related this story to me and I passed on this message to Brian, who was touched by her story and thought that he did remember walking to work with her.

June was very supportive of Brian and me during his illness and after his death via numerous messages and we thought how lovely that people care who we don't really know. Thank you, June xx.

Brian certainly made a lasting impression!

I used to walk to work with Brian every morning when I was a 16 year old; being a young teenager, Brian was the apple of my eye!!!

It was lovely talking to him as it was my first job and he helped me so much as I was a shy girl in those days, and he helped me a lot to gain my confidence, although sadly I didn't get a date with him.

He worked in a clothes shop on the high street in Grantham, and I worked in an accountants office, but the half-hour walks every day meant the world to me. Then sadly he went away, and I don't ever remember seeing him again, but he never went out of my mind...
Young Love, eh?
RIP Brian xxxxxxxx
June Pulfrey

Personal songs composed by Billy Walker

Babs' Words:

Billy spoke to me about when he used to go to the shows in which Eddie Cochran appeared and remembered our Brian well and was impressed at the joy and happiness which radiated from the music. He wrote this as a tribute to Eddie and Brian. Thank you Billy x

Brian April Theme re: Eddie Cochran

It was on an Easter Sunday Morn when I awoke to find you gone=The unchained summer melody=Ripped within the heart of me=Eddie Mr guitar son =They always say=The good die young=Mister Bassman that was my role=I shared your light=you reached my soul=the Sunday papers headlines news=No more Eddie summertime blues=My tears did flow=I could hardly see=There's one thing=They can't take from me=My cherished Cochran memories=It was an Easter Sunday morn=My heart awoke=To find you gone
Xx

Song with Lyrics Words and Music
Me & my rainbow=My guiding light=Bluebirds & melodies eternal flight=Above the bass line=Blue harmony=Oh me and my shadow and me=Forever entwined =In step with each other=Two of kind=Like sister and brother devoted eternally=Me and my shadow=Brian Locking and me
Billy xx

Twin tribute/memories by Margaret and Diana:

Our first meeting with Brian ("Licorice") was at Lytham St Annes, (near to where Sir Cliff Richard's bungalow was at that time), then again in Manchester 1961 where Brian was wearing an off-white suit, and he told us jokingly that Sacha Distel (famous singer at that time) wanted to buy it from him!

After that we did not meet him again until 2000, where we went to a show at the London Palladium, and also, we met and spoke with Brian Bennett who complimented us on our smart appearance.

When we went to the *Shadowmania Weekend* at Lakeside, Frimley, Brian came to our table and made himself known to us and we chatted, and we showed him earlier photos we had taken of him, then he gave us his address where he lived in Wales. We were thrilled on our next visit to S*hadowmani*a, that Brian dedicated his musical rendition of "Sleepwalk" to us and said, "This is for Diana and Margaret who you know as 'the twins' on table 64." We were thrilled!

Several time we went to the 100 club and supported him there and met several other musicians (including Vince Eager). We even travelled over to France to support him there and had a wonderful time with "Lic" and his great friends, Bernard Broche and his wife Jacques, and Cliff Hall. We were made to feel very welcome by the French fans.

Later on, Brian would play gigs at the *Scarborough Music Gala* weekends, and we would take him for trips out around there and have meals together. It was great fun. We would all stay at Ingrid and Clive's Majestic hotel and have lovely intimate musical evenings in the hotel, after the brilliant music gala concert.

We would also travel up to see him at the *Newcastle Music Gala* weekends and to Grantham when he was appearing at shows with Vince Eager and other musical friends and we would meet up with his sister and brother-in-law, Babs and Dave. It was always a good time.

We travelled over to London once with Brian and his companion Pat to the Hackney Empire to see the *UK Music Hall of Fame*, then we all stayed at a bed breakfast together.

Many years later we went to *Marty Wilde's 50th Anniversary Show* at the London Palladium and "Lic" invited us to the after-performance party and we met Marty, Bruce Welch and others, and Babs and Dave.

We always enjoyed chatting to Brian, and particularly when he was seriously ill. We were very upset that we could not attend his funeral because of coronavirus restrictions.

RIP "Lic". We miss you and thank you for being such a good friend since 2000 when we met up with you after a long absence. We will never forget the good times and your wonderful musicality (particularly playing the piano in the lounge at the Lakeside complex prior to the *Shadowmania Concert*), also, you playing bass and your wonderful harmonica at the many different pubs and concerts and encouraging other artistes, particularly the Foottappers in Derby, and meeting Jim Walters who showed much kindness to us both.

RIP "LIC". WE WILL NEVER FORGET YOU.

Letter from a Shadow fan sent to Brian during his illness, from Rodger Meachem

Babs' words:

Brian had never met Rodger or knew of him, but he was thrilled when I read this letter to him and to read the booklet that Rodger had sent.

Dear Brian,

I hope that things are getting a little better for you and you are getting a little stronger as the days go by. Dad used to tell me "Rome wasn't in a day, son, take things slowly." Strange thing to tell me though. I've never been to Italy, but I think I got the drift, I did go on to do a lot of things slowly, though!

I have enclosed a copy of one of the few books that were ever produced about the Shadows, it just so happens that it features a certain "Licorice" Locking alongside your mates. I used to read my own copy of this when this first came out in 1963, then when I'd finished, I would start all over again.

I would have been 14/15 years old and lived for the Shadows records, then only 45s and 33 and a third of course, and I had every record on a rolling order at our local record shop. In those days you could go into a booth and listen before you bought. I never bothered with the Shadows records, just went in, paid my 6/4d and walked out happily with the latest Shadows record tucked up under my arm.

The problem was when I got home, straight upstairs, dansette record player on full volume of course, and then dancing round my bedroom with my guitar strapped on, pretending I was one the group. Lasted around a minute I would guess before Dad came crashing in, "RODGER!! WHAT THE BLOODY HELL ARE YOU PLAYING AT? YOU CAN HEAR THAT ROW HALFWAY UP THE STREET, WILL YOU TURN IT DOWN!!"

That of course would not have been a request, so half volume until Dad went to work. Mum was so much easier to get round, and after a while, she too became a Shadows fan.

I can still see her now, in her domain, the kitchen, asking me the name of the last record I had put on. She forgot straightaway of course, but more than once I caught her humming "Wonderful Land" or "Guitar Tango". Then she would ask, "What was the name of that tune Rodge? I really like that."

I think she was almost as excited as me and my brother when we came to see you at Bristol Hippodrome all those years ago in 1962; Dad probably suffered in silence as he was unable to control the volume for once!

I still think that no Shadows anthology exists and there is very little historical material around to tell the Shadows story as it should be told. The greatest instrumental group to ever walk the walk, I shall continue to campaign to get that put right.

In the meantime, Brian, I hope this booklet will bring some lovely memories for you, I know I still dip into it all the time, and I still recall the thrill of your music, which in my humble opinion is timeless.

Thank you for the brilliant videos that Babs posted on Facebook, they will be treasured, you've still got it, sir, and I send silent applause to you.

As I have said more than once, you were part of my youth and a big part of my growing up with my love for music, and I thank you sincerely,
Get well soon Brian.
With love and sincere wishes.
Rodger

Brian enjoying Rodger's letter and tribute poster.

Letter (?) to Brian from? (whoever is responsible for this?? Ha ha!)

Ugglebarnby & Fryup Idle Working Men's Club
Cemetery Road, Ugglebarnby TZ3 4U2

"Dear Mr Lacking,

One of my fellow Committee members had them to be in Scarborough last weekend when his wife persuaded him to pay for two tickets to see your Cliff Richards and the shadows show. If it's any consolation to his wife Doreen, said she enjoyed it but didn't care for the bald man in the red shirt who kept coming on and interrupting the music. Doreen's husband Wilf said the bit he enjoyed best was the mouth organ playing as it made a change from all the noisy drums and banjos (I think he meant gitars)!!

Anyway, the reason I am writing to you is that Wilf got talking to some bloke after the show who said him & you do a turn in the pubs playing the gitar and mouth organ, and he gave Wilf to understand you work cheap. Is that right? If it is then you might just be what we're looking for to do a turn at our local produce show annual prize and bingo night. We did have a promise from Enid Entwistle that she would bring her accordion and do us her "Songs that lost The War" (in German of course), but her keys have got stuck together owing to some excess vinegar when pickling her gherkins and we're really stuck. You and your oppo Ian Harpic (is that his stage name?) could go down really well if you keep the noise down.

Ours is a little club but friendly (in its own way) and Doreen thinks that those old tunes you played at Scarborough would go down real good once folks have had a few. Do you bring your own mouth organ? I only ask because once a bloke turned up to do a magic act and he didn't bring any stuff with him. He kept asking the audience for stuff like five-pound notes and watches, which he never returned, and it all got very ugly, and we had to lay on the tripe supper a bit sharpish. As for payment I am orthorised by the committee to ask you to name your price (within reason of course - I think £30 between you is not unreasonable in this day and age). The turn usually does two lots with bingo in between and there will be an interval while we oction the veg. (turns are NOT allowed to bid!!)

As we will be paying you above the odds, we will expect you also to be the judge of our Ugly Granny contest. It used to be Glamorous Granny, but we only ever had 1 entrant and she won every year, even though she was nothing to write home about. Since we made it the Ugly Granny contest there's been no end of old biddys wanting a go. I trust you've got your own suits and that (denims are not allowed in the concert room). If you want the opportunity of playing at this prestijius club, please let me no soonest.

Your faithfully

C. Kilmarnock

(Cyril Kilmarnock, Hon. Sec.)

Think someone here was the culprit of the above letter!?
Scarborough Shadows music band.

Babs' words:

This reminds me of one of Brian's many favourite jokes.

Can you think of a name of a fish beginning with the letter K and ending with the letter K?
No, I can't think of one what is the answer?
The answer in Kilmarnock!
But that's not a fish!!
But it is a Place (? Plaice?)!!!

Another joke (usually, an announcement from Brian on the stage).
Would the owner of the car with the number plate RGOLMSTBXVCQEK 1357908642 please move your car ...
It is blocking the entrance!!!
(Sorry!)

Talking of comedy! Many friends and ourselves have first-hand experience of Brian's fun and sense of humour, and we could possibly fill another book up with various stories, tales and antics, especially with two of his good friends, Kevin and Brenda Harris.

Kevin is the DJ and compère for many Shadows music clubs and conventions in England and is a rhythm guitarist too, and has formed his own musical group, the Diamond Geezers, who combine Shadows/instrumentals and comedy within their group and regularly play (Covid-19 allowing), in their local club, and any other events they are invited to.

They have been friends with Brian for many years and Brian has often stayed with them and the humour and banter between them is infectious!

Two stories here are related here by Kev, but if anyone ever meets, Kev and Bren, sure they can relate many more!!

Kev Harris's words:

I do have a reputation for doing things in a hurry at times, without thinking it through (as Bren will tell me!) and Brian always found this hilarious and would pretend to groan inwardly then keep reminding me of what I had done!!

I picked "Lic" (Brian) up from Piccadilly station, Manchester, but before I could get in the car, I dropped the car keys down a drain grid! Brian groaned in despair and pretended to walk away, whilst finding it very funny to watch me as I got down on my hands and knees, then lying on the pavement to stretch my hand and arm down the drain to try and retrieve the keys from the drain, and in a blind panic about losing my car keys!

Thankfully, it turned out that the local council had cleaned the drains, and I was able to put my arm down quite safely and retrieve the keys much to my relief, though wasn't sure at the time!!

We then set off to our local club to do a sound check for the show that we were performing later that night, then drove back to our house in Manchester where we then lived.

Unfortunately, we had a dodgy sunroof in our old Volvo, which would keep falling on our heads as it was not secured properly, and as were driving back, the sunroof fell onto Brian's head. And as it was quite a long journey back, poor Brian had to hold the roof up with his middle finger till we got home, but oncoming cars thought Brian was making a rude gesture, and they would stick their fingers up back at him!

At this point Brian very dryly reminded me of how he had played at the Hilton in Canada, the London Palladium and various other top places, then he said, "I can't believe this is what it's come to... me, holding your sun roof up with my finger!!"

After all that, the evening gig went brill, and we celebrated with drinks, as his sister Babs and her husband Dave were staying with us too. The alcohol flowed very quickly, and whilst Brian was climbing upstairs to his bedroom, he slipped and banged his head on the stair, sustaining a large bruise on his forehead. I got the blame for this too and he never let me forget it!!

Story two

Brian stopped at our place before going up to the *Newcastle Gala Shadows Club* weekend, and on the way up to the venue, forever the gentleman he was, he said that if there were any gaps or difficulties with the events being organised there, (as I was the organiser and compère), he would help me out, and whilst I was busy compering at the venue, this is exactly what happened! There were two stages at the venue, one for solo artistes and one for groups, and it got very busy and frantic for me as I was trying to organise all the different acts, and Brian saw I was struggling so he leant over my shoulder to offer me assistance, and I misread the situation and said quite angrily to him, "NOT NOW 'LIC'!!"

This was my downfall, as every time I spoke to him on the phone or met him, he would repeat these words to me, and he never let me forget it!!

Brian was such a talented man and one of the loveliest charismatic gentlemen that you could ever wish to meet, and a great ambassador for the Shadows. We loved him to bits, and he is very sadly missed.

GOD BLESS YOU OUR SPECIAL FRIEND.

Kev and Bren xx

Kev Harris and Brian

Kev and Bren xx

The big yellow truck tour

Tribute by Ritchy Rich:

Lead guitarist of The *7abulous* Shadows with Jimmy Jemain (Cliff Richard tribute and winner of *Stars in Their Eyes*) on *The Golden Greats Tour* and *An Audience with… Hank and Bruce* tribute nights, with Steve and Ritchy (until Steve had cancer and Ritchy had a brain tumour).

At *Shadowmania* the The Big Yellow Tour Truck would be seen in the car park at Frimley Green Lakeside venue. (Who could miss it!) As Bruce Welch (the organiser of *Shadowmania*) passed by it his eyes popped out. "Look at the size of that." was heard as he drove past it.

Brian was a visitor in it, and we took him for a ride out. We would talk about how luxurious it was compared to the double decker in the *Summer Holiday* film, which I thought was funny, then we had a deep conversation about the truck as I built it from scratch as it was an ex-DHL delivery truck. I did all the decals on it and bought the registration number 66 TFS as a tribute to the Shadows, and I handmade all the interior and the gold discs, Oscar and tour passes!

I have a massive collection of the Shadows and Cliff's sheet music and Brian signed and played my Fender guitar.

Brian's private joke was, if Jet Harris had signed it his signature would be bigger!!

I will never ever sell the Fender Precision bass guitar as Brian's fingerprints are still all over it.

I also have a 1949 Gibson guitar. My music mentor Big Jim Sullivan lived near me, and he was the last person ever to play this.

Both guitars are now my works of art and are kept very safe. Xx

Personal message:

Nick (doctor bass) Smith (bass guitarist with Genesis Connected)

I started playing bass in 1982 and growing up with my dad being a Hank soundalike, meant that the music of the Shadows was a large and important part of my childhood, and all the Shads' bass players were massively influential on me as a young bass cadet!

I turned fully professional on bass in 2001 after spending 12 years working in the computer software industry and I got to work with Shazam which are a well-known Shads tribute band.

We did one of the *Shadfests* up in Blackpool in around 2003 and this is where I first met Brian! I'd never met him before but myself and my late partner Andrea went down to his room, and it was like we'd always known each other; we immediately got on very well and that was the start of a very dear friendship with him.

We went on many shows together sharing the bass duties with tribute bands such as Shazam, the FootTappers and the Shadowers, and Brian, Andrea and I did some pub gigs near his lovely home in North Wales.

He lit up any room he entered and would always give me such a hug when we met up!

I remember picking him up from Grantham railway station in my car to travel over to Nottingham together to do a theatre show – we got talking and I said, "Brian, when you joined the Shadows in 1962, you were the most famous bass player on the music scene at that time!!!" He smiled, looked at me and said, "You know what my son, I've never thought of that!"

But he was, and I for one treasure the memories of him and miss him dearly.

We will see him again one day, love you my musical dad!

Nick

Babs' words:

I for one have experienced Nick and Brian's closeness in personality and musical talent, and Nick and Brian I believe are the only bass guitarists to play a double act of playing "Nivram" at *Shadowmania 2012* with the Shadowers tribute band, and on many other occasions with Brian. (See YouTube.)

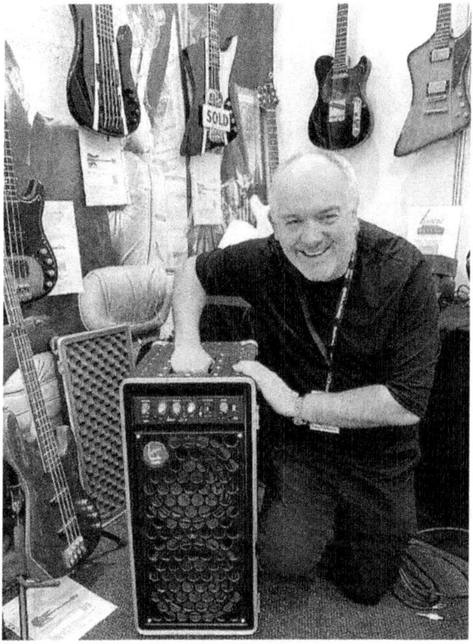
SOLD

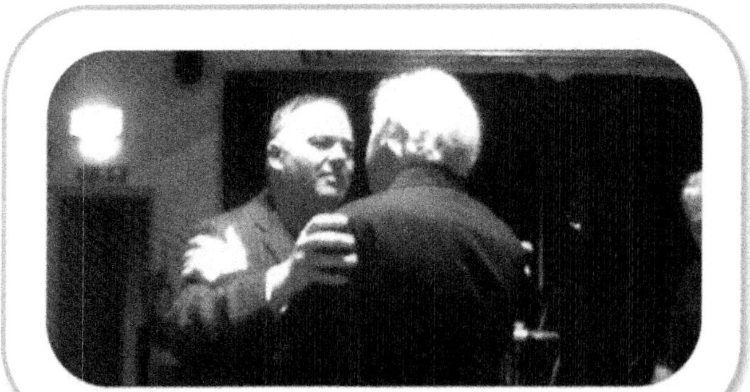

The Shadows Danish festival

ShadowDania in Nyborg, Denmark

"Harmonically Friends" by Biorn Arnesen:

The first time I ever met my old hero, Brian "Licorice" Locking, was backstage after the show at Bruce Welch's *Shadowmania* in 2006.

Six years later, at *ShadowDania* in Denmark, I was lucky to meet him again. After that we met every September at the Danish Shadows festival *ShadowDania* in Nyborg, Denmark, where myself and eight other Shadow lovers drove the long way by car from Norway via Sweden to Denmark to see and hear real Shadows music. We even brought our Fenders and Voxs with us so we could play together at the *Friday Social* at the hotel where we stayed.

I remember the first time we asked Brian to join us back in 2012, and just had a five-string Fender bass to offer. Brian said, "sure I wanna play with you," so we quickly had to remove the fifth string from the bass so Brian could play it.

The *Friday Social* was a jam session in the hotel basement, which turned out to be in one of our rooms, so the name turned out to be The ShadowDania Basement Jammers, where Brian was our honorary member, as he was in the Danish Shadows Club.

We could play for hours, and Brian really loved those evenings, playing the old Shadows stuff with friends from all over Scandinavia. I remember asking him to play "Dakota", and he gave us a wonderful version of the tune there down in the basement.

In 2015 my music pals and I started a new band called The 2i's Coffee Band with the name taken from the 2i's Coffee Bar in London's Soho, where it all started for Cliff and the Shadows back in 1958.

"This is the second-best band name I have ever heard," Brian told us, and the best was for sure the Shadows!

Brian was always "Top of the Bill" at *ShadowDania*, performing his Louis Armstrong songs and his magical harmonica renditions of many a great song, including "We have All the Time in the World" and "Time to say Goodbye".

Brian also loved to go on stage and do some Shadows numbers on the bass with the other bands. We asked him to play "Dance On", "Foot Tapper" and "Dakota" with the 2i's Coffee Band, and he said yes immediately. Brian then told us it would be first time he did a duet performance of "Dakota" on stage, ever.

We quickly made up an arrangement, with me playing the first verse on my chromonica, whilst Brian did the second verse on his. Then we shared the bridge and the third verse, with Brian doing all his magic fill-ins.

That evening on stage in Denmark, duetting "Dakota" with "Licorice" will be forever the highlight of my musical career.

The author of this book, Brian's sister Babs Wilson, and her best friend Gill Pugh, also used to come over to Denmark to make friends and see Babs' famous brother on stage. We used to ask Babs and Gill to do the "Apache" dance on stage with the 2i's Coffee Band in our final number "Apache", and it always turned out to be a great success every year.

The last time we met Brian and played beside him, was at *ShadowDania* in October 2019 when he joined the 2i's Coffee Band on harmonica for the old Wee Willie Harris's number "Rocking at the 2i's", which is the Coffee Band's signature number.

Brian and I became close friends after our many rendezvous in England and Denmark, and I used to call him on the phone every 22nd December just to say, "Hello how are you?" and after that having a long, nice chat. But now he's gone for ever, and it's with a sad heart I write these lines.

Rest in Peace Brian – I know we'll meet again.

Biorn

The 2i's Coffee Band (Norwegian Shadows music/and instrumental artistes)

Tasty (Norwegian Shadows/instumental band) with 2i's Coffee Band

All good friends at with Gulle at the Villa Gulle Hotel, Nyborg, Denmark.

Playing "Time To Say Goodbye".

2i's Coffee Band's "Apache Girls", Gill Pugh and I (Babs)

A letter from Brian to Gijs Lemmen

Gijs words:

Brian was a real friend of mine for about 20 years!

Many times, he visited our home and the studio (GFC workshop) in Sliedrecht (The Netherlands) and stayed mostly four days to do recordings with me.

And later on, we did it again, four days and so on, and so on.

We made six CD albums. We recorded about 44 or songs together at our studio.

Also, we did some touring through Germany and The Netherlands together and with our GFC studio band.

Always great fun.

Brian's letter and words:

Dear friends and fans.

I must say that to play music with Gijs Lemen (guitar), Elly Swets (bass) and Ad Vos (drums) at the Theatre Sybold in Dordrecht, is one of the best times I have had for a long time. It truly was very memorable for me.

As I walked in the theatre, it had a good atmosphere, and warm feel about it.

Everything was there, a nice grand piano on it which we had to move. We started setting up our amplifiers. Everything was happening, it was like a beehive.

Jan Bek, the manager of the theatre was so good, looking after us with endless cups of coffee and tea, which I enjoyed very much.

He was included in our musical program and sang Donovan's "Universal Soldier", which went down really well.

The theatre was full, I had a lot of belly laughs with members of the bands, telling silly jokes with each other.

I must say the audience were very warm and enthusiastic with our music, including a very nice standing ovation at the end.

And wow, that meal we had afterwards!

But I truly had a wonderful time staying at Gijs and Rika Lemmen's home and enjoyed their company very much (not forgetting that rice and chicken and salad meal with a fantastic chocolate drink afterwards). Brilliant!

I look forward very much to coming again in the near future when Gijs, Elly and Ad I will enjoy playing for you once again.

Once again, THANKS.

Gijs LEMMEN and Brian xx

Italian friends (from Rome), Piero and Teresa Cioccooni

Babs' words:

Wonderful message received after Brian's passing from Piero and Teresa. I did not know them, but when they sent their pictures, I immediately recognised them from Brian's photographs, and when I had previously tried to find out who they were!!

Teresa's words:

We were very sorry to hear the sad news of Brian's passing in October last year and would have liked to send you our deepest condolences then, but unfortunately we didn't have your address or know how to contact you. Pino Pini, one of the prominent members of the Italian Shadows community has just told us that you have been in touch via Facebook, which is why we are now able to write to you.

Wherever he went Brian was loved by everyone he met. His warm broad smile was unique, and he had a wonderful way of remembering everybody We were friends with Brian for many years, and with our children in the 1990s, we also met his friends, Denis and Pat George.

Brian came to stay with us in 2000 and music filled the house from morning till after midnight!! That year he was guest of honour at the *Italian Shadows Convention*, and we'll never forget the drive from Rome to Rolo when we had the misfortune to get stuck for several hours in the worst traffic jam you can imagine on a very hot day!! What a nightmare!! But Brian kept our spirits up with his harmonica and tales of his days with the Shadows and with Marty Wilde and the Wildcats.

It was on that journey that we had a welcome break in Florence and Piero took the super photo of Brian with his bass guitar in the Piazzale Michelangelo with the city in the background.

We met Brian in England, after I was visiting my family in Sussex. Brian, Pat and Dennis were on holiday in Warnham and we met them at the Sussex Oak pub.

Brian had the most wonderful smile... always!

Brian played for many local venues including hospices and clubs. We remember when we were in Wales, and on the Saturday the *Denbigh Music Festival* was on. Our children, Michelle and Daniel had a super time taking part in the races and having their faces painted whilst we enjoyed the wonderful musical entertainment given by Brian and his friends.

Brian was one of the kindest, nicest people we have ever met, and a great musician, too. You must miss him terribly and we are sending you our deepest sympathy and much love.

Piero and Teresa Cioccoloni

Brian 'Licorice' Locking

Story and tribute by Ian and Joy McCutcheon of Shazam Shadows tribute band:

(*Hank Marvin Concert* at the London Palladium 16th June 2002)

As I recall it was a warm summer Sunday in June 2001 and we had managed to purchase six tickets in the centre of stalls row C to see Hank Marvin. This had been advertised as *Hank's Final Solo Tour* and the Palladium show would be his last ever solo performance.

"Licorice" was one of the six for whom we had purchased the tickets and to finish off the evening we were all staying at the Drury Lane Moat Hotel.

We arrived early on the Sunday afternoon at the hotel and "Licorice" decided to take us on a walk around his old stomping ground within the area of the 2i's Coffee Bar.

As we walked along the various streets, "Licorice" was telling us stories of how he had lived literally hand to mouth in those early days often being fed from leftovers at the end of the evening by the more friendly café owners.

Before we headed back to the hotel to ready ourselves for the evening we decided to locate exactly where the Palladium was for later.

We arrived just near to the stage door entrance where we could see some fans eagerly awaiting the arrival of Hank. Just at that moment someone a short distance away shouted "Look, it's 'Licorice' Locking!"

At this point he was pretty much mobbed by autograph hunters. I don't think he expected the adulation but nevertheless he responded immediately in his usual relaxed manner talking freely to everyone.

That was quite an unexpected moment and something I will never forget.

General:

I first met "Licorice" at Blazers nightclub in Windsor where the Shadows were performing their *25th Anniversary Concert* in 1983, and he was an invited guest.

It was just a "Hello" and he signed my programme. I never thought at that moment I would be playing guitar on countless shows with him in the next few years!

Whilst working with him I can recall many happy times, perhaps the most memorable being the immense number of stories he could relate about his life in show business.

The more things he would recall the more I wanted to ask him.

He would talk about his appearance on *The Royal Variety Show*, the filming of *Summer Holiday*, his time on tour with Marty Wilde, Eddie Cochran, touring America with Cliff Richard and the Shadows at the time of the Cuban missile crisis etc., etc. The stories were fascinating and he would recall everything in tremendous detail. There are so many more things I would still love to ask him.

I was always amazed by his easy-going nature and boundless energy when it came to anything musical. I remember trying to keep up with him running along a road one night in Germany about 20 years ago, when we had been asked to play a few items at an informal party a few hundred yards away from the hotel and we were late. I remember thinking I hope if I reach his age, I am fit as he is!

For me perhaps the most precious time would have been recording and producing his *Harmonically Yours* album in my studio. We spent many happy hours on that project.

"Licorice" would arrive here on a Thursday or Friday, and we would work solidly through until the Sunday lunchtime at which point, we would go out for a well-deserved Sunday lunch.

I can't imagine how much air he must have blown through his various harmonicas during those sessions, but the brilliance of performance on that instrument was totally consistent.

Finally, I have to say that it always felt a tremendous honour and privilege to work with "Licorice" and the memory of those times is something I shall always treasure.

Ian

Brian "Licorice" Locking
Harmonically Yours
Digitally Recorded

Warwick Shadows Club and Ian and Joy McCutcheon

Denbigh male voice choir

Tribute by Richard Thompson:

On asking Brian (when in his seventies) on reflecting back on his career, did he feel there is still something to achieve? His answer was:

"You bet Brian Locking wants to play and appear in concert with a male voice choir. If possible, a Welsh one."

"Believe me, I am not making this up."

With the passage of time Brian moved to the beauty and tranquillity of North Wales.

He attended the Denbigh Folk Club on a regular basis where the affable and talented multi-instrumentalist would perform on guitar and harmonica. Always ready to offer advice.

The all-time favourite song in the male voice choir repertoire has to be Joseph Parry's "Myfanwy".

A mournful, yet melodious story of unrequited love. Loved by audiences for well over a hundred years. Of course, it's in the repertoire of every male voice choir in Wales and beyond.

Furthermore, Brian knew this song and loved its beauty and structure, and he could play it on the harmonica and turned up on our practice night.

His plaintive and haunting interpretation was utterly enthralling. He played the first verse as a harmonica solo, and the full choir joined in for the second verse.

The chemistry worked, and Brian appeared with us at our next three concerts and each occasion "Myfanwy" was a resounding hit. Brian also enjoyed the whole experience. I swear I saw him wipe a tear from his eye. Music created that emotional effect.

Unfortunately, we never got to record "Myfanwy" with Brian at any of the concerts, but we really enjoyed them, and we invited him to be guest artiste at the choir's annual dinner. He played the harmonica and bass guitar for well over an hour. Classic hits again from his Shadows days.

Thanks for casting a shadow with us Brian.

Possible last interview of Brian by Adam Coxon (interviewer and friend):

William Blake said, "The most sublime act is to set another before you."

Whether it was his faith, his spirit or a product of both, the Brian Locking that I knew was selfless, fascinating and indescribably gracious. He was humble, gentle and grateful.

The first time I met Brian, he hugged me like a friend, or a brother and I'll never forget that. He radiated a warmth and familiarity that I felt I had somehow met him before.

I'd been sitting in the stalls at the beautiful Guildhall Arts Centre in Grantham watching Brian and Vince Eager rehearse for two hours. Whilst watching these two master craftsmen rehearsing for their show that night, I suddenly thought, these guys have known each other for 60 years. How incredible to have been friends for that length of time and then to still be playing music together.

The last time I spoke with Brian was a very short time before his passing, when we conducted what I believe was the last interview that he ever gave. He wasn't feeling well but he didn't want to go into it. We had an arrangement as far as he was concerned, he was sticking to it, and if that was his wish then it was mine.

After we'd had a great catch up, we got down to business and Brian "Licorice" Locking came to life. Brian's life experiences were as rich as his heart.

Brian Locking was certainly a blessed man, but I'm blessed to have encountered him on my journey. A journey which I often struggle to understand myself. Whenever I think of Brian and his unwavering faith to his religion, to the people he loved and held dear and his kindness to every person he met, I am inspired, and comforted Brian was a dedicated man, and his spirit will live on in all those who were graced by his humanity.

Every leaf that grows will tell you, what you sow will bear fruit, so if you have any sense my friend don't plant anything but love.

Rumi

Farewell to a friend
(Horst and the convention team, Dr Jochen Barsch and Ursula Kunz, Switzerland):

On 8th October the following message arrived:
"Brian 'Licorice' Locking fell asleep peacefully at 7 o'clock today.

I passed on this sad message by mail and wrote about it.

Brian has enriched the programme of our *Shadows Music Convention* in Verden, 17 times. Additionally, we met Brian in Eindhoven, Tilburg, Breda, Kornwestheim, Oslo and Nyborg, and during this time we became friends.

Lately his age has become noticeable and in the last weeks he was taken to hospital where he died now at the age of 81.

Brian, we would like to thank you for the many wonderful performances that will remain in our memories.

Rest in Peace!
Horst

Brian "Licorice" Locking

In 1977 Brian Bennett released a song on the LP *Rock of Dreams* which he had dedicated to his late friend John Rostill, "Farewell to a Friend". This title immediately came to my mind when it became know that John's predecessor in the Shadows, Brian Locking had died after a long illness.

Brian was dear to many of us during the 17 years he was regularly with us in Verden. His humanity based on deep Christian faith, his kindness and his modesty were an absolute rarity in show business. The end of his life was foreseeable for a long time, but still his progress is a shock.

I would like to take this opportunity to say that we were united by a very intensive friendship and a contact that went far beyond the musical. Therefore, I am deeply sad to say goodbye to a friend.

If there is Heaven, in which Brian believed so strongly, then he will be allowed to occupy a beautiful place there. And if the saying is true that a person is only dead when nobody remembers him, then Brian "Licorice" Locking lives on.

RIP, my friend.

Dr Jochen Bartsch

Those who know Brian well will miss him very much.

I met Brian in 1967 here in Zurich, where he was a guest of friends of mine. Together with his buddies Malcolm and Gordon, the four of us drove back to London in a car. There I got to know him as a friendly and humorous person. Star's airs and graces seemed strange to him.

After 46 years we met again at *Swisshad* in Bosingen. He didn't know that I was invited, and of course there was a big hello!!

Brian would certainly have liked to have lived much longer, but even he could not prevent his complaints.

He had no fear of death, because he knew that he would then be free of pain in a sleep-like state. He also believed that Jesus Christ had the power to resurrect him here on earth. Not in this corrupt system, but on an earth after Armageddon, when all evil and harmful things will be removed.

In the meantime, may he rest in peace.
Ursula Kunz, Switzerland

Brian and Ursula Kunz

Personal message:

Alison Petifor
Tony and Brian

They first met at the Shadows Club around 2005.

Dad had had his liver transplant in April 2004 and spent most of the year in hospital.

Dad first picked up a guitar, brought by his mom and dad, when he was 12 years old, being inspired by the Shadows.

He taught himself to play by ear and his first song was "Wonderful Land". Dad had a lifelong love of music and the guitar. He was in a band the 4 Embers, and he was just 15 years old when he started in the band.

His illness really affected his ability to play the guitar and he had to give it up which he found very distressing thinking he may never play again.

After his transplant, it was amazing. It brought him back to life. He could remember everything he'd forgotten and picking up a guitar again gave him a new lease of life. This is when he joined the Scarborough Shadows Club. It was at one of their galas where Dad first met Brian.

It was a great honour for Dad to meet Brian and become his friend. The Shadows were my dad's childhood heroes.

He also met Bruce Welch and Brian Bennett at *Shadowmania* at the Lakeside in Frimley.

He met Steve Valentine, who introduced my dad to Bruce and Brian. It was through this friendship that he also met Hank Marvin on *The Final Tour* in Manchester.

Brian knew what my dad had been through with his health, and was always willing to play at fundraisers for my dad's Charity "Ray of Hope": a charity supporting the Liver Unit at St James's hospital in Leeds.

He did a number of these, and one was in Halifax for the launch of a book: *Small Town Saturday Night* by Trevor Simpson. The book was all about the 60s music scene in Halifax and the bands who played there, including my dad's band, the 4 Embers.

Brian met Trevor at another fundraising gig with my dad at the Norland club Halifax whilst raising funds for a policeman's baby, born with a brain condition.

Afterwards, they all went back to Trevor's house. Trevor is a massive Elvis fan and has written numerous books, some of which have been endorsed by Priscilla Presley, who he knows personally. Trevor has a lot of Elvis memorabilia, including a Wurlitzer Jukebox containing 100's of 60s singles. Brian thoroughly enjoyed his time at Trevor's house. Trevor gave Brian a copy of his book.

Brian also played at my dad's 60th birthday party which was an honour for everyone there. My dad and Brian became very good friends My dad always rang him to see how he was and how he was getting on.

It was extremely sad for all of us when we discovered that Brian was ill. We couldn't even visit him when he was in a convalescent home in Leyland, two miles from where I lived, due to Covid-19. My dad was obviously devastated when he succumbed to his illness.

I once had the pleasure of cooking homemade pie and peas before another fundraiser gig at the Wheatsheaf pub in Leyland, near our previous home.

He regaled us with many stories about his time with life on the set of *Summer Holiday*: a film I have always loved. I could not believe that I had such a star in my home and felt a little embarrassed that I had fed him corned beef and onion pie. He very graciously said he enjoyed it.

He was a true gentleman, kind, generous with his time and my dad was honoured and greatly appreciated his friendship.

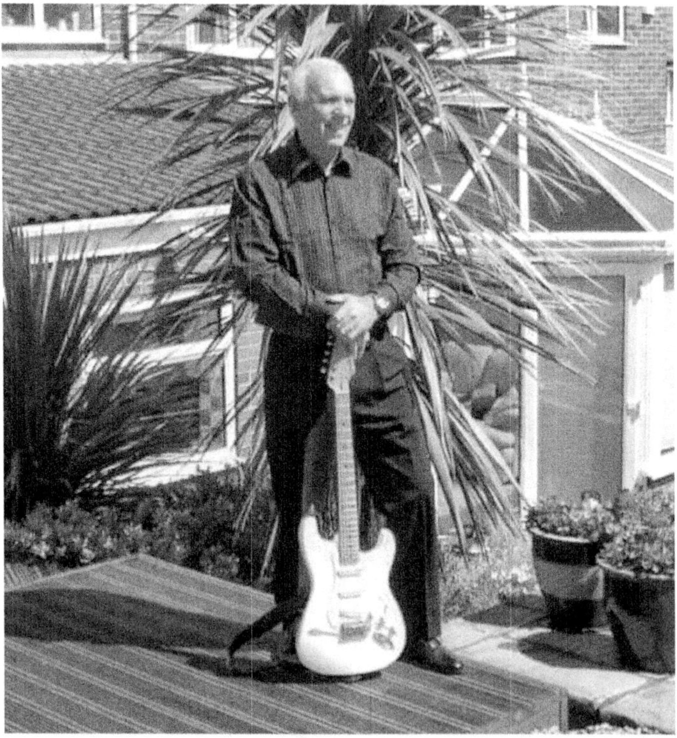

When in France, my friend Brian Locking

Tribute by Bernard Broche

Like all Shadows fans, I discovered Brian Locking on the record covers in 1962, after Jet Harris left. I was 12 years old. Then John Rostill took over as the Shadows' bass guitarist. And so no more news from Brian.

In June 1990, I created the fan club "Les Amis de Cliff Richard & The Shadows" and I also created the magazine *Established 1958*.

When I wanted to buy a Burns Marvin guitar, I got in touch with Barry Gibson, and that's where the first contact with Brian was made. Barry called me up on day and said, "I'll put you through to someone who will make you happy!" "Hello, I'm Brian Locking, do you remember me? (of course), that's why I'm calling you, I'm applying for my pension and I need to know which tracks I recorded with the Shadows and Cliff Richard."

I was 12 years old. But since then, I have a lot of archives and I can find everything without any problem!

Then with the fan club, I started to organise the *Cliff Richard & The Shadows Festival* in the Paris area every year since 1991 (in Vif later).

Brian had come for the first time in 1997 to Nogent-sur-Marne with Barry Gibson's band Local Heroes: Phil Kelly, Alan Jones, Jet Harris, Cliff Hall, Brian Locking, Clem Cattini, Keith West and also Bruce Welch.

Brian and Bernard Broche

French friends

Babs' words:

France was like a second home to Brian and he travelled regularly over there to stay with his very good friend Bernard and his lovely family in their home in a most beautiful area of France.

Brian would regularly be taken on sightseeing outings and would play on stage with Bernard's tribute group The Blue Shadows and many other prominent musicians in France.

The Cliff Richard and Shadows fan club is a very popular club, and their members are extremely supportive of Cliff and the Shads and organise prestigious concerts, regular newsletters and books. Brian just loved being with his friends there and learnt how to speak and sing even in basic French. He loved the people and their language.

One huge highlight was a prestigious concert in Paris, where he and Shadows' keyboard player Cliff

Hall, played and recorded a most beautiful and moving musical arrangement called "Life Story". This was written by Jerry Lordon (of "Apache" fame) but was never played or recorded.

Jerry's wife Claudine very kindly gave this to Brian and Cliff, and they played it at the special concert in Paris where Claudine Lordon was guest of honour.

Everyone just loved this, and of course especially Brian, Cliff and Claudine.

On Brian's passing there were some wonderful tributes devoted to him in the *Fan Club Magazine* of which a copy was kindly sent to me by Bernard Broche.

"Tribute To Brian Locking" (*Fan Club* magazine 12/2020) (Translated from French):

Hello friends,

It is with great sadness that Bruce Welch announced to us by telephone the death of Brian Locking on 8th October at 7am following an aggressive cancerous tumour of the prostate. His funeral took place on Monday 19th October at 2pm in Wales where he resided. We were able to attend the 40-minute ceremony via the internet.

It started with the broadcast of "Nights in White Satin" played on harmonica by Brian (you can listen to it on YouTube; Brian performed this title at *The Swisshad* in 2013). I can tell you that this was very moving to hear it like this, followed by the original Shadows' "Apache" to recall that he had been the band's bassist in 1962 and 1963. A moving message from Hank Marvin was then read. After the praise for Brian and his faith, this ceremony ended with Brian on his harmonica, "It's Time to Say Goodbye". Brian Locking leaves no one indifferent, thank you to all those who speak out about him by giving him a tribute.

Claudine Lordon:

Tribute to Brian Locking.
To speak like our friend Christian Sicot in the *Fan Club Review*, There is no need for superlatives to express how I feel when I think of you. You were and will remain for all of us, this showbiz gentleman who combined simplicity, kindness and charm with a remarkable musical talent imbued with poetry and marked by style and creativity, both on guitar and harmonica. Personally, I remember being deeply moved when you played "Lifestory" unaccompanied with just your dexterity as a harmonica player. You knew, indeed, how to perfectly express all the passion contained in this composition. I understood at that moment, why your interpretation of "Lifestory" with Cliff Hall was so perfect and it would most certainly have pleased its author, who used to say, "I don't ask for much in life, only perfection."

Brian, thank you for everything.

I will always have the fondest memories of Brian in my heart.

Warm Regards.
Claudine

Cliff Hall:

May I write this little tribute to Brian Locking for the magazine. I have fond memories of playing with Brian Locking every time we visited you for the fan club. And of course, Brian and I have worked together several times with Jet and Bruce's Shadows at Lakeside's *Shadowmania* and which has always been a show we all loved. Brian has never been happier than on stage with his harmonica or playing bass guitar. He still had that big smile on his face. We recorded "LifeStory" for Claudine (Lordan) recently and we had a great time. Claudine was so happy with the recording. Brian's friends will always remember him with great affection, I know that. So, Jo and me, friendships. XX

Bernard Broche:

At the age of 70 he had climbed on foot to La Bastille (where there is a cable car in Grenoble) with me, visited the Chartreuse convent as well as the liqueur distillery of the same name in Voiron and often said to me, "Chartreuse day!" after tasting it.

I met Brian Locking for the last time in Paris at the Cidisc on Saturday 1st February of this year; he had appreciated Thierry Liesenfeld's book *Chansons Magiques* where he saw unpublished photos of himself. Back in Wales, and as for a long time, we called each other several times a month. His health changed abruptly from the month of June. Brian was a remarkable man, for his talent as a musician, but also for his kindness, his eternal smile, his way of being on stage. A particular anecdote from 2010; Brian wanted to learn Charles Trenet's song "La Mer". So, word for word, I taught him this song which he wrote in phonetics so as not to forget it and once he got home, it was like a rehearsal on the phone, "The Sea we see dancing..." A song that he was able to interpret with Guitar Express then at the *Festival de Vif* and also at one of Bruce Welch's *Shadowmania* shows by dedicating it, "to my French friends". I always keep the emotion of a title (premonitory?) on the harmonica for "The Last Farewell*"* which he performed with us and which you can listen to on my Facebook page. There were other concert projects in Dijon, and an album was planned with a symphony orchestra, all that will not happen. As a souvenir we have his CD albums, including one *Returning Home*, recorded at Warren Bennett's studio, funded by the fan club and published by Magic Records. But there are still some tracks recorded with Cliff Hall, during the *Festival de Vif 2011* and "The Lifesto*ry*" recorded in studio in January 2020 with Cliff Hall, thanks to Claudine Lordan. Brian leaves us this wonderful souvenir to be released, thank you my friend!

Armand Ronin:

Some memories in memory of Brian "Licorice". I discovered Brian Locking after reading *Disco-revue* and *SLC* from November 1962 and on the cover of the LP *Out of The Shadows*. Eighteen months and a hundred Cliff/Shadows titles later, "Licorice" is slowly disappearing from the limelight. On 17th May 1997, in Nogent-sur-Marne, I finally met "Licorice" and had him sign a photo showing him playing "Nivram" at the

Olympia in 1963. Surprised by this shot, he asked me to send him a copy. He would thank me warmly, by mail. I saw him after at *Shadowmania* and at the festivals organised by the French fan club. At Bernard's home on 18th June 2018, I had the chance to chat with him for several hours. He spoke of the beginnings, the Wildcats, the Krew Kats, Vince Taylor and February 1960 where he accompanied Gene Vincent and Eddie Cochran and ended his memories with *Summer Holiday*. I find him one last time at the end of the concert at La Fouillouse on 13th April 2019, with Guitar Express and Ricky Norton. Thank you for all these good times spent with this charming boy and his legendary kindness. Bass player, talented harmonica player who has rubbed shoulders with all the big names in English rock and who has just joined them in "Rockers Paradise". Emotion and Respect. "Dakota" for ever. (He is even on a Johnny Halliday LP *Salut Les Copains* from the 60s.)

Emmanuelle Grasset:

It's hard to imagine we won't see Brian again at festivals. He will leave a huge void. His mere presence lit up the room. His talent, his smile, his humour and his kindness will be missed. Fortunately, we still have many photos and videos to remember these wonderful moments spent in his company. We especially think of his sister Barbara and her husband Dave, and of you Bernard and Helene for the loss of a dear friend.

Ricky Norton:

Cliff Richard wrote down his sadness and gratitude after the news of Brian "Licorice" Locking's passing. I had this privilege from the top of my humble journey to have met this charming and oh so talented man. I have often transformed myself into and manage to succeed in organising trips to France where he was the spearhead. Concerts at his side, a legendary studio session too, when I think about it today, I say to myself, "How lucky to have lived these wonderful musical and friendly moments with him and Guitar Express!"

In 2010, we had the biggest party ever at Petit Journal Montparnasse. Bobbie Clarke and Brian Locking together and all our guests for an Eddie Cochran special! What pride, what honour! He loved to play the harmonica and there it is beyond talent; it is a symbolic journey to the land of beautiful melodies. Eddie was supposed to come back and play the blues with him, Brian was telling me that. And they would have done this duet, guitar-harmonica. Fate decided otherwise. Brian spent time with me, with us, during his stays in Paris, France. We took care of him like a member of the family. He loved us. With each phone call that we exchanged, he took the time very quietly to name the friends and I had to pass on to everyone his deep friendships. Brian Locking dazzled us with his positive flamboyant presence, as he dazzled the history of music, from the Wildcats, Lonnie Donegan to Eddie Cochran, Gene Vincent, Vince Taylor for his legendary "Brand New Cadillac" and the Shadows of course!

I am sad because Brian is exceptionally human and of rare truth. His forever.

Philippe Massa:

It is with great sadness that I read your message informing me of the death of "Licorice". I will keep a very good memory of this very kind and warm man whom we have met together on many occasions. I keep the photos preciously and videos of his visit to Richard where we played together with Alain Pistono, and also of our concerts at the restaurant Blanc Desir. For me he was the most endearing of the Shadows because he was very approachable and not proud at all. I didn't have much opportunity to approach the other members of the group. You, Bernard, you have of course been able to forge more links with all the Shadows because of your position as president of the fan club. Finally, time passes, and we get older, also more ahead of us, they are all approaching 80 years. "Licorice" will remain in my fond memories for a long time. Good health to you and Helene. Friendships.

Gilbert Migliori:

Brian, I was happy to know you and to have been able to accompany you during several concerts. You kindly told me one day that on drums I should not be a follower but the leader of the group, so I got on it and I thank you for it, but above all I saw that you Brian, you were shining with a light that I would call divine and that had touched me, thank you.

Richard Fourre:

Brian was not only a talented musician who played with many well-known musicians, but he was one of the most adorable and sympathetic people I have met, thanks to the fan club created by Bernard Broche. It was a good musical relationship with which I shared unforgettable moments of conviviality. And it was a privilege for me to share these moments with him. Brian you will always stay in my memory.

Alain Pistono:

Brian "Licorice" was one of the icons of my youth, along with the Shadows! He was a simple, outgoing and very sympathetic man. Thanks to friends of the club, I had the opportunity to meet him and even to play in his company, going on to interpret together the bass solo of "Nivram". A great unforgettable shared moment!

Stephane Le Galloudec:

I am also saddened, especially since without this damn corona we would have replayed together last May. Thanks to you (Bernard) I had the privilege of playing with Brian at Vif and Cohade. Playing the music of the Shadows and playing it with one of those who was in the band is a game changer. We no longer copy when we play with Brian, we are in the sharing, in the moment. We play with energy and heart. He was very present on stage, and he was alert to everything that was going on. He noticed all the subtleties and details when we played together, we were very complicit in our moments, and he also had this immense class of not letting on about the mistakes that each of us could make. I actually learned a lot from him live on stage, and without rehearsals, without prior focus. His attitude, his stage presence, his sense of sharing, his alert spirit, his joy of being, his tolerance for imperfection, all this radiance of knowing how to live and knowing how to play whilst remaining smiling and generous brought me and changed my look at life in general. It was a great, great experience. We had, as you know, recording projects together. I'm very sad that they didn't come to fruition.

Jean-Claude Hugues:

Hello friends. Like all of us, it is with great sadness that I learned of Brian's passing. Bernard had informed us that he had been hospitalised for a urinary problem (probably prostate cancer or bladder or both) and that he would recover and come back to us in good shape and still very dynamic. Alas no. My wife and my children were also very touched, especially since Brian came to us twice in Lyon, accompanied of course by Helene and Bernard. More precisely (I noted it) on 5th May 5th and 16th June 2014. It was the occasion to make him taste the local cuisine: gratin dauphinois, classic in Lyon, chicken with lemon, good recipe of the "mothers" Lyonnaise but also Creole cuisine (Mauritian tuna, pickled vegetables), grilled meats with Greek rirani (oregano). What good times! Walks in the Parc de la Tête d'Or in front of our building in the Cité Internationale, great discussions with my perfectly bilingual son and daughter as opposed to my supermarket English. Nobody is perfect! We saw Brian several times thanks to Bernard's concerts in Grenoble and Saint Étienne and the last time in Valence. Always with great shared pleasure, I think. And then also at Bernard and Helene's in Cohade in June 2018. A few mini harmonica concerts; you know his virtuosity on this instrument! What a beautiful time! Friendships to all. That we meet again from time to time despite the passing years. Happy New Year's Eve everyone with Cliff's latest CD for example! And despite the current vicissitudes. No worries it will pass! Do not forget with the flu vaccine is still time and the Covid-19 vaccine when it comes out (it's the doctor talking!). We are fragile at our age! Tchao!

Marc Charpentier:

On our late Brian, we have lost an exceptional person of extraordinary human and musical sensitivity. His kindness could be read on his face, always simple and ready to do the beef with us, he will always remain in our hearts. Rest in peace my dear Brian we will meet again one day. Best regards from Guitars ZZ.

Jean-Claude Foy:

I have just received your magazine which is very pleasant, but which saddened me to learn of the death of Brian Locking, who had marked the musical period with the Shadows; it's sad!! I wish you a lot of courage and all your team, you are great! Very great friendships!

Patrice Bastien:

Needless to say, it is with great emotion and great sadness that Guitar Express and I learned of the passing of Brian "Licorice" Locking on 8th October 2020. Even though we knew that he had to be operated on and that he had had a stroke at the end of last June, before returning to the hospital intensive care again at the end of September, we were far from imagining that he could leaving in such a short time. And the frustration of not being able to attend his funeral other than through the internet link because of Covid did not help matters. "Licorice" was a bit like a big brother for us. We were both joking about the fact that the first time I saw the Shadows live in Paris was in '63 on the Olympia stage with him on bass. Now having the chance, barely 40 years later, you have trouble realising that whoever happens to be next to you on stage was that of our favourite instrumental group, that for my part, you had seen at the Olympia in 63! Besides being a very good musician, Brian "Licorice" Locking was a lovely person. Always in a good mood and happy to play. And more Shadows than "Licorice", in his compromise on stage, you die! Thank you again for giving us a lot of advice both musical and how to stand on the stage. Our other great memory is during his recording in the studio, with him on bass and harmonica for the titles of a Ricky Norton single. Needless to say, "Licorice"'s disappearance is a big void for Guitar Express. Worse! It is an era and real shared pleasure to come together that are disappearing. Rest in peace Brian. You will stay in our hearts forever.

Bob alias "Big Araf":

My dear Brian, when I joined the group Guitar Express, I had no idea that meeting with you would have been possible. Like millions of people, I never imagined this event could ever happen, even more in concerts where I would be by your side. In addition to this shared happiness, I keep in the depths of my heart our sarcastic exchanges full of English humour as well as having instituted for each of us a little password to guarantee our little complicity. Dear Brian, knowing that one day we will all have to pass in the next room, we organise a beautiful concert with all those who have already made their home there. Your friend Bob.

Alain Bertrand:

My first physical meeting with "Licorice" took place in 1998 in Tours, for a tribute to Henri Leproux; the decor of Golf Drouot had been recreated. I had only been with Guitar Express for a short time, when I was asked to go hold the rhythm, alongside Barry Gibson and Brian Locking. Alain Jocou was on drums. It was, however, hot to burst under this marquee, but I was there on stage, to the right of "Licorice", to play the Shadows music!!!! I saw myself in '63, holding in my hand the 45 rpm where this new bass player appeared, whom we nicely nicknamed "the redhead". He immediately put me at ease, with his eternal benevolent smile, and his natural simplicity. Since this first time, on many other occasions, he guided us, advised us, calling us by our respective first names as soon as he arrived at the meeting place. On the stage it was always advice, quite simply a little glance, with "the step" that had to be taken at such and such a moment. I think he loved us, Guitar Express and Ricky, with whom there was a natural symbiosis!! Ricky called him on the phone, and he was coming! Quite simply, Ricky has much more sophisticated English than ours!! With the CD *The Meeting*, recorded in November 2010 (ten years ago already), it was a great moment that we lived. Our last meeting took place at the Cidisc, on 1st February of this horrible year. We had played with him the day before at the Jazz Café, Montparnasse. He was still enthusiastic, even though he seemed a bit tired to me (maybe that's my impression). Shortly after, containment arrived. No more concerts, our last one was on 8th February in Alsace, with an unforgettable welcome. No more rehearsals, each in his corner, trying to continue living "normally" until 8th October. Farewell "Licorice", our Big Brother, so beloved by all.

Jurg Beerhalter:

My first meeting with Brian was at Bernard Broche's in Vif in May 2011. A very friendly discussion followed, and Brian even played a few notes on my diatonic Hohner harmonica. I showed it to him and to my surprise he took it from my hand and pulled out sounds that I didn't know existed. I also saw him at Crolles where he played with Bernard's band the Blue Shadows and we had a great evening. After one of the concerts of the *Fan Club Festival* in Vif we went to the restaurant for lunch with Brian, Bernard, Helene, Jacques Debize (also now deceased) and his wife Genevieve. During a concert at the Petit Journal de

Montparnasse he very kindly lent himself for a small, filmed interview intended for Bernard, because he was not there that day. What good memories.

Best friendship, Bernard Broche, fan club, Auvergne, France.

Arrivée de Brian Locking et Ricky Norton avec P-A Delpierre
(Shads In Breizh 2018)
Photo B.Diebold ©2018

Brian, and Emmanuele Grasset

Claudine Lordon (wife of Jerry, who wrote "Apache"), Pat George, Bernard Broche and Brian in the garden at Brian and Pat's bungalow in North Wales.

Helene Broche, Brian and Claudine in the bungalow, North Wales.

Brian's last theatre performance

2nd November 2019 at Newport's Riverfront Theatre in South Wales

Talking Music: Brian "Licorice" Locking and Maurice Woodcroft – Guitar Moods and a Shadow.

Brian was joined on stage with Newport-based musician, Maurice Woodcroft, who for many years, fronted the Shadows tribute act, Bungle Flint, and he featured Shadows numbers in his solo act.

Brian was interviewed just before this show by Andy Howell, who asked what people could expect from the forthcoming concert. His answer was:

"It'll be very nice! There'll be a bit of mood music, singing, strat stuff, all the golden oldies really, like "Apache", "Atlantis", "Guitar Tango". There's a lot to get through but I'm going to do a lot of chatting in between with some stories that perhaps nobody knows about!"

Story and Tribute from Maurice Woodcroft

Brian Locking and the 7-ton parrot:

Little could I have known way back in the early 60s that the bass guitarist with the Shadows, who played on hits like "Atlantis", "Foot Tapper" and so many others, would become a close friend in my later years.

In 2003/4, I was busy organising the South Wales Shadows Club's *Shadows Extravaganza* at the Hilton hotel in Newport.

I invited Brian along as a special guest (Bruce came to our second event), and he stopped over at our house that weekend. He was a delight, and we were thrilled when he agreed to be a guest with my Shadows tribute band Bungleflint at a show we were planning at the Market Theatre, Abergavenny.

During his stopover with us, we spent several hours together playing some well-known standards such as "Autumn Leaves" and "Misty" with Brian on harmonica and myself on acoustic guitar. This mutual love of this style of music had already brought us together. The other thing that brought us together was our silly sense of humour!

One afternoon, we were relaxing in our lounge, recalling some of those schoolboy type jokes, when I recalled a particularly daft one from my past. I asked Brian, "What's green, lives in trees and if it fell on you, it'd kill you?" Already giggling, Brian replied, "I don't know, go on, tell me what it is…"

"A 7-ton parrot," I replied.

With that, Brian burst into a fit of giggles and then uncontrollable laughter, as he slowly slid off the settee onto the floor, like the Salvador Dali watch painting before curling doubled up on the carpet in hysterics!!

From that moment, every phone call between us began with Brian asking, "Is that the 7-ton parrot?"

It also cemented a very special relationship that I have and always will hold dear to my heart.

In late October 2003, I was devastated by the sudden death of my beautiful wife Joy. Brian rang me almost every day to see how I was coping and the incredible love he gave me over the following months helped me through one of the most difficult periods of my life.

Like everyone who knew him, he was a gentle, caring man with a deep love of music and people. I would never have thought that the two-man show we did together in November 2019 at the Riverfront Theatre in Newport would be his last professional gig.

Like all who have met and known Brian, his passing has left a massive hole in our hearts and lives.

RIP Brian.

Maurice Woodcroft

'Guitar Moods'...
(Featuring Maurice Woodcroft)
Background Music with Style

HI BRIAN!
IT'S NO GOOD YOU KNOW,
BOOKING YOURSELF INTO
HOSPITAL TO AVOID DOING
ANOTHER GIG WITH ME!
SERIOUSLY, I'VE BEEN
THINKING ABOUT YOU SINCE
I HEARD ABOUT YOUR OP.
I REGARD YOU AS A VERY
SPECIAL FRIEND SO REST
ASSURED I'M WITH YOU
IN SPIRIT AS YOU GET BACK
TO GOOD HEALTH.
 HAVE YOU FOUND ME THAT
CHROME PLATED WHEEL NUT
FOR A ROUTEMASTER YET?
I'M STILL WAITING!
 I'LL TRY & GET TO SEE
YOU WHEN YOU'RE FEELING
BETTER.
 LOADS OF LOVE &
 BEST WISHES,
 FROM,
  MAURICE
 ('THE 7 TON PARROT'!)

UNSUSPECTING VICTIM OF THE 7 TON PARROT!

SPLATT!

HOME TOWN OF GRANTHAM

Babs' Words:

Brian always loved to come back "home" to Grantham and when he came over to visit us it was usually combined with visiting familiar places of his childhood and he would reminisce with his stories, and he was so very fond of visiting Witham Place where he spent many happy times.

The street is now demolished, and flats are built near the river where the top of the street was (and the little bridge!), but shortly before the little houses were demolished and were empty, Brian took a sentimental trip around there, on his own, and walked through the passage into the yard where our house was... No 5. He said he was deeply moved and stayed there for a long time thinking about his memories, times with our parents, me and Rob, grandparents, aunties and uncles, cousins and his very good friends and all their antics, and he said the wall of the passage to the yard still had the marks on where he and his cousin had thrown their rubber balls hard around the passage and making them ricochet off the passage walls!!

He loved to visit his friends too in the town and would spend hours talking with them. Dave and I would drive him around different areas where he wanted to visit and look at and, of course, there was usually a show planned in town, or a party where he would be entertaining, as it would be his reason to visit (apart from seeing me and Dave).

He always had remained in contact with his musical friends in town: Vince Eager (Roy Taylor, ex-

Vagabond then later a singing star in his own right) and Trevor Leeson (ex-member of the Mersey Beats and famous in Grantham for being in various other local groups e.g. Dawn and The Deejays etc., and still very popular and in demand in Grantham, around Lincolnshire and further afield in many clubs and different venues, with his great talent/versatility with guitar and vocals). Another friend, Terry Carey is a roofer by trade and supplements his job with entertaining, with his drumming talents and great singing voice and also visits many venues and clubs in Grantham and around Lincolnshire.

There are many more musicians in and around Grantham and Brian loved to be around them and play alongside them, and other musicians were often invited to play alongside them in town, usually in the iconic Guildhall Arts Centre.

Peter Donegan, Chas (from Chas and Dave), Tommy Bruce, are just a few to visit, and other groups too, Brian was always loved and very popular with Grantham residents, and he loved to be with them and chat with them. There are many stories that can be told about the pre-London days and there is always someone too willing to talk about them. Brian just loved being in town and was hoping to eventually move back but unfortunately his illness took over his plans.

St Wulfram's Parish Church, Grantham

About TREVOR LEESON

- Trevor started his musical career as a member of "The Rebels" Skiffle group in 1958. By 1961 he was touring American Army bases in France as lead-guitarist with "The Pontiacs" with whom he also played at the famous "2 I's" coffee-bar in London's Old Compton Street, where many of the better-known stars of the day, including Tommy Steele and Cliff Richard, made their debuts.
- In 1965 his new group, "Dawn and the Dee-Jays" (they were called "groups" then, not "bands") recorded a single, written by Trevor, which was released on RCA records; the same label as Elvis! Two of the sessions-musicians hired to assist were Jim Sullivan, lead-guitarist for many years with Tom Jones, and Jimmy Page, who later went on to form Led Zeppelin.
- In 1969 he was recruited into a group from his home town of Grantham, called "Gingerbread", in the capacity of bass-guitarist. Gingerbread were regularly featured on BBC Radio 1 on shows hosted by the likes of Terry Wogan, Jimmy Young and Tony Blackburn. After completing two seasons in Douglas, Isle-of-Man with Gingerbread, Trevor went to St.Helier in Jersey, where he worked on a show alongside "The Merseybeats". It was soon after this that a vacancy occurred as bass-guitarist with The Merseybeats and Trevor was invited to take up the post.
- In 1974, after a couple of very enjoyable years with the "band" he decided to embark on a solo career. Since then he has chalked up a remarkable CV, working on shows with The Electric Light Orchestra and Ken Dodd, to name just two from a very long list. As well as his excellent vocals and solo work on the guitar, he can also give out plenty of comedy patter where required.
- He has now completed well over fifty years in entertainment and has absolutely no intention of retiring from the business he has revelled in since day one!

Trev Leeson, MerseyBeats

Noel Wallis (Grantham music promoter for many local entertainers in Grantham for several years, including the Vagabonds), Ken Dodd (well- known comedian and entertainer and friend), and Trev Leeson

Peter Donegan (son of Lonnie donegan), great entertainer in his own right and appeared at a special show at the Guildhall Arts Centre, Grantham, alongside Brian, Trev Leeson, Vince Eager and many more local entertainers/musicians.

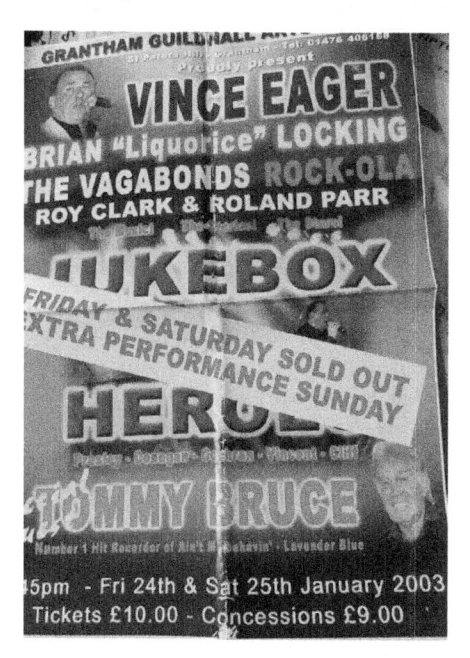

Trev Leeson and Vince Eager performing at Grantham's Guildhall Arts Centre and Ballroom. Yearly concerts were performed there for local charities and Brian often appeared here as well. These were organised by Roy Wright, a prominent organiser of many entertainment events in Grantham and well known for the yearly events of Grantham Carnival and Party in the Park, all great exciting events which raised much cash for worthwhile charities in the town.

Roy Clarke, Brian, and Vince Eager (Roy Taylor), the original Harmonica Vagabonds, still giving a good show! (Or blow?)

Sylvia Chantry, my beloved friend from early schooldays and who has supported me so well throughout Brian's illness and passing, and is always a great friend XX. She has always been a great fan of Brian's as many more have been in the town, and who are very proud of him.

One of our many parties, our ruby wedding party in Grantham, with wonderful friends and family, and entertained by Brian, Trev Leeson and Vince Eager, plus Shadows tribute musicians and friends. (Me (Babs) with my lovely brothers Robert and Brian.)

Ruby wedding party with our very FIRST meeting with long lost cuzzies (now there is a story to be told !!) who travelled all the way from New Zealand to meet us, Debbie Davis and Helen Schofield, with Brian and partner Pat, and our very good friends Kevin and Brenda Harris.

Another wedding anniversary party for us on our golden wedding! We were entertained very well with Brian and Trevor Leeson and it was Brian's last party entertainment before he fell very ill.
Brian with my school friends, Christine Clark, Gillian Hodgkin and Diane Baker.

Brian's wonderful friends, Carole and Trevor Leeson. They have always supported Brian so well during his stays in Grantham and stayed over with them many times. Brian always loved being with them (as with all his friends), and Brian and Trevor's rapport and entertainment was truly AMAZING!!

**Brian's favourite meal ever with us was... DAVE'S
LEGENDARY BREAKFAST!!
"Breakfast is served... is a knife and fork required sir or will
this shovel be more appropriate ?!"**

Brian absolutely adored Dorothy (Dot), Dave's mum, as she did him. He would always play especially for her, and her favourite song was "Danny Boy" (as played for her many years ago by her husband, Bill, Dave's dad).
Brian always entertained and we had regular harmonica entertainment with our mum, brother-in-law Paul Gerrard, brother Malc Wilson and sister Jan Gerrard. XX

EMBASSY THEATRE
Skegness
Lincs
IN AID OF THE LINCOLNSHIRE FLOOD VICTIMS
WITH AN ALL STAR LINCOLNSHIRE CAST
YELLOW BELLIES UNITE!
Brian "Licorice" Locking
Shadows Bass Guitarist
Vince Eager
Rock 'n' Roll Legend
Ali James
Everybody's Favourite
Trevor Leeson
Ex Merseybeats Guitarist
Tickets Only £10
Terry Carey
Dynamic Vocalist/Drummer
Your host is Mr Skegness - Chris Tucker
Wednesday 3rd July 2019
Tickets available from The Embassy Box Office - Grand Parade - Skegness - PE25 2UG
Box Office Tel Number - 01754 474100 or book online at - embassytheatre.co.uk

Brian's last ever public performance at the Embassy Theatre in Skegness, Lincolnshire, in aid of the Lincolnshire flood victims, in Wainfleet, whose homes, and surrounding countryside were devastated by horrendous flood water. The show had a full house and was magnificently performed by all the Grantham musicians. (Kevin Harris lives in Blackpool, but he was "adopted" as a Grantham musician/entertainer, being a very good friend of Brian's!) An excellent show and compered by the famous Mr Skegness, Chris "Tuc" Tucker, known as "The Man in Red", and the owner of East Coast Radio *Coastal Sounds*, and being the media/producer and presenter.

TREASURED TIMES WITH OUR SHADOW

Babs words:

Whenever Brian visited us, or we visited him, it was always special and always fun-filled and we would catch up on all news, and he always entertained us with his music, whether at our many parties, celebrations or wherever he had been with us.

His harmonica was always in his pocket, and we have been musically entertained at our home, in our garden, in our car, in other people's homes, cars and gardens, in cafés, pubs, shops… and anywhere and everywhere!!!!

And when he was not playing, he would be talking to anyone who wished to talk to him with absolutely NO restrictions on time and loved to listen to everyone else's stories, and he always had a pen in his pocket to sign autographs for anyone who wanted them. We are sure many of his friends can vouch for this!

Many times, this happened to us, and usually in a very busy venue where Brian would sit down briefly for a drink and something to eat, then someone spotted him, or he spotted someone he knew and went over to chat. By the time he had finished chatting, he had forgotten where he had put his drink and/or let his food go cold, so of course very often, when we left the venue, he was very thirsty and hungry.

Usually late at night by then, so thank goodness a McDonald's was open or something similar!!

The next morning Dave would cook him a huge fried breakfast, which he absolutely loved and very quickly demolished!

Brian always loved his food and could eat huge meals and we always packed him up with sandwiches, crisps and cakes for his journey back to Wales or London, which he would immediately consume as soon as he sat down on the train.

For many years Brian was only able to visit a few occasions in a year, as he lived many miles away from us in Wales and he worked part-time and travelled around a lot on his musical journeys and in between time he was devoted to caring for his dear friend and platonic partner Pat, with whom he shared his life and Christian faith over many years. He shared the house that Pat and her husband Dennis lived in, in London, not long after he had left the Shadows group and had been good friends with them whilst he was with the Shadows.

Eventually, they all made the decision that they would buy a property and move up to live in beautiful North Wales (in an area of outstanding beauty), away from the hustle and bustle of city life.

Pat and Dennis always cared for Brian, and we loved them very much, and are eternally grateful to them for their love and companionship of Brian, and they would all often come and visit us in Grantham. Our parents loved them and were so happy that Brian was well cared for, and with lovely and trusted friends.

They lived a good life in North Wales and were very happy and had a lot of friends there. They were always very busy being involved with work and their religion and always helping others.

After many years Dennis sadly died, but Pat and Brian continued to support each other in Christian care and platonic companionship, along with their two cats Tommy and their adopted wildcat friend Scoot, who were very precious to them both (even though Brian was allergic to cat fur), and they both had the best care they could have had (the cats!). Brian worked in a veterinary practice alongside other types of work, and he and Pat were always very fond of animals and supported pet charities.

Unfortunately, Pat tragically had a severe stroke several years later and was hospitalised, which was devastating and there was little hope of recovery. Brian would catch the bus daily up to the hospital to visit her, and although she was unable to speak or barely move, Brian would sing and play his harmonica to her, and the rest of the staff and patients in the hospital!

Brian was obviously very upset and coped very well with the bungalow and caring for himself, as previously Pat had always been in charge of everything and would guide Brian, but on her passing he managed to cope, with help from his friends and his congregation. Brian, in his role in the Witnesses' faith as a qualified pastor, bravely and lovingly organised and presided over Pat's funeral service, and he also played music there at the reception afterwards. She was a wonderful lady and sadly missed, as was her dear husband Dennis, to whom she had been devoted.

Brian bravely lived on his own afterwards in their bungalow, and although he struggled at times at being on his own, he was always uncomplaining, and he had the support of his faith, friends, us and his music, and adjusted well to living on his own.

We always hoped that he would move back to live in Grantham to be near us, and he was very excited at the thought when he visited, but circumstances were, at that time, that he felt committed to stay in North Wales for a little longer.

Brian never liked to complain, even when things were starting to go wrong in his body, and he would not think to ask for help, but carried on regardless and we were not aware of the extent of his health problems, as he wasn't either! He chose to ignore and carried on regardless of his health. His priority was his music, his friends and his faith.

We spoke regularly via phone, for long periods of time, and on his last visit to us to play at our golden wedding celebration with his close musical friend Trevor Leeson, he appeared to look tired and had lost some weight, but he insisted he felt fine and remained cheerful.

One day, shortly after he had returned back to Wales, he rang us and told us had been admitted to hospital after suffering what he had thought was a stroke! This turned out to be Bell's Palsy which was a paralysis of one side of his face, causing his mouth to droop and difficulty with eating and drinking, and he was unable to close his right eye.

He was discharged from hospital, and we rang and checked him twice daily via phone and were ready to go over to be with him, but he insisted that he was coping OK, getting correct treatment and eating and drinking well, although his eyesight was bothering him. We insisted he get help from an optician and possibly a consultant referral from his own GP. (This he did, but had to wait for appointments, then Covid-19 came along which delayed everything!!) His eyesight continued to deteriorate, and he was told by his optician that nothing could be done and he still had to wait for a consultant appointment! He did get an appointment eventually, but this happened whilst other problems were occurring within his body. (Just before his death, he was officially diagnosed as being registered blind from macular degeneration!!)

Unfortunately, problems were occurring with his bladder, but still he did not complain, and he was referred to a urological consultant, and was receiving some support from friends and neighbours, he told us, but did appear to be struggling, so Dave and I made plans to go over and stay with him.

A date was set for an investigative operation at the local hospital, and Dave and I were due to go Wales for when he came out of hospital, but unfortunately things went wrong after the operation and poor Brian developed sepsis and was extremely ill and required intensive medical care.

We liaised with his consultant, and the hospital daily, and spoke to Brian when he was able to speak. The staff told us he was making a good recovery and was transferred back to a ward and receiving rehabilitation and would be allowed home.

On hearing the good news, Dave and I immediately drove over to Wales prior to his discharge to prepare his bungalow and intended to stay with him as long as we were needed.

We liaised with his lovely neighbours, Jim and Sharn, who were very helpful and had supported him too by caring for his two cats, Tommy and Scoot, as Brian really worried about them.

On arriving to his home, we were extremely upset and shocked, as it showed the extent of his struggles to cope on his own! Of course, it was through no fault of his own, and he tried his best and he would never complain.

He was brought back from the hospital by his very good friend David Sylvester, who had been absolutely wonderful in helping to take him to his various trips for appointments at the hospital and anywhere else he needed to go to. But to see him on his return from hospital we were very saddened by his appearance and his fragility, and loss of weight.

We cared for him and his home and his cats and it was such a huge pleasure for us all to be together again.

We organised all the care he required at that time for his personal care, physio, etc., and his appetite returned after famous breakfasts again (much to his delight!), and regular nutritious meals and drinks were taken well, in small amounts, including a very enjoyable glass of port as a night cap!

Brian started to look so much better, and we had fun and laughter and music again as he practised his music in his beautiful conservatory overlooking the wonderful scenery of the Welsh hills.

Letter and cards and phone calls came pouring in for him and he was deeply touched by them, and we met and spoke to some of his neighbours and many friends, who were all so lovely.

Plans were made for recuperation in a rest home that was run by his Jehovah Witness faith, and he really looked forward to the care he would get there and hoped it would give him a boost with his care and rehabilitation, and Dave and I planned we would come over again on his return and for as long as we were needed.

We also started to make plans for a possible move back to Grantham, so he could be near to us and his many friends, and he was extremely excited about this, as were we!

Unfortunately, as plans often do, they went astray, and without going into details, after his return from his rehabilitation home, his health took a rapid turn for the worse, but thanks to his neighbour Jim, he was re-admitted back into hospital, despite Brian's protests that he would be OK!

Thank goodness he was in hospital getting care, and we dashed over very quickly back to Wales and managed to be with him during his last few days of care, in intensive care and that wonderful hospice, St Kentigern in Saint Asaph, North Wales.

Brian was fully aware and understanding of our presence, and prayers and words and gentle hugs were lovingly exchanged. When he was transferred over to the hospice, all the staff knew him well, as he had entertained and supported them there on several occasions in the past, and they loved him very much. Their care was just amazing to Brian and to us.

Special thanks to ALL who cared for Brian and us in his last days of his illness and the support of Brian's friends through the many messages sent.

Special thanks to Brian's wonderful friend David Sylvester, who assisted Brian on his many journeys to the hospital and appointments prior to his admissions, and also took him out on special journeys.

Also, a special thank you to John Barrows, his very good friend, who would visit or phone him every single day at his home during his illness and took us all out for a wonderful day out in his car through the beautiful countryside of North Wales, despite suffering from his own disabilities. It was extremely pleasurable to Brian and us, and when in hospital and the hospice, John visited him every day when we were not there and would ensure Brian's favourite classical music was played.

At 7am on 8th October, on his heavenly journey, the nurse told us that Brian was comfortable and peaceful and listening to the music of André Rieu.

Brian's words:

Don't forget, you are my one and only and I love you very much... and Dave, I give you a bunch of fives, and look after my shoes!!

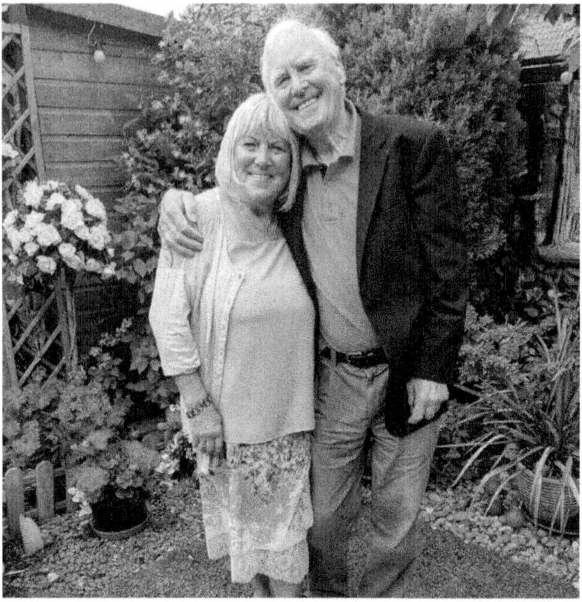

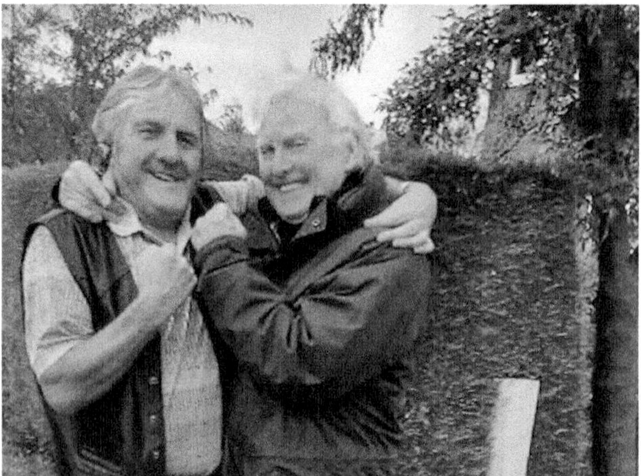

NIGHTS IN WHITE SATIN
Justin Hayward

Nights in white satin
Never reaching the end
Letters I've written
Never meaning to send
Beauty I'd always missed
With these eyes before
Just what the truth is
I can't say anymore
'Cause I love you
Yes I love you
Oh, how I love you
Gazing at people
Some hand in hand
Just what I'm going through
They can't understand
Some try to tell me
Thoughts they cannot defend
Just what you want to be
You will be in the end
And I love you
Yes, I love you
Oh, how I love you
Nights in white satin
Never reaching the end
Letters I've written
Never meaning to send
Beauty I'd always missed
With these eyes before
Just what the truth is
I can't say anymore

Yes, I love you
Oh, how I love you
Oh, how I love you
YES, I LOVE YOU.

Brian's home in North Wales with his devoted cat Tommy (Ginger) and the ferrel friend Scoot who adopted Tommy and Brian!

LOVED AND NEVER FORGOTTEN

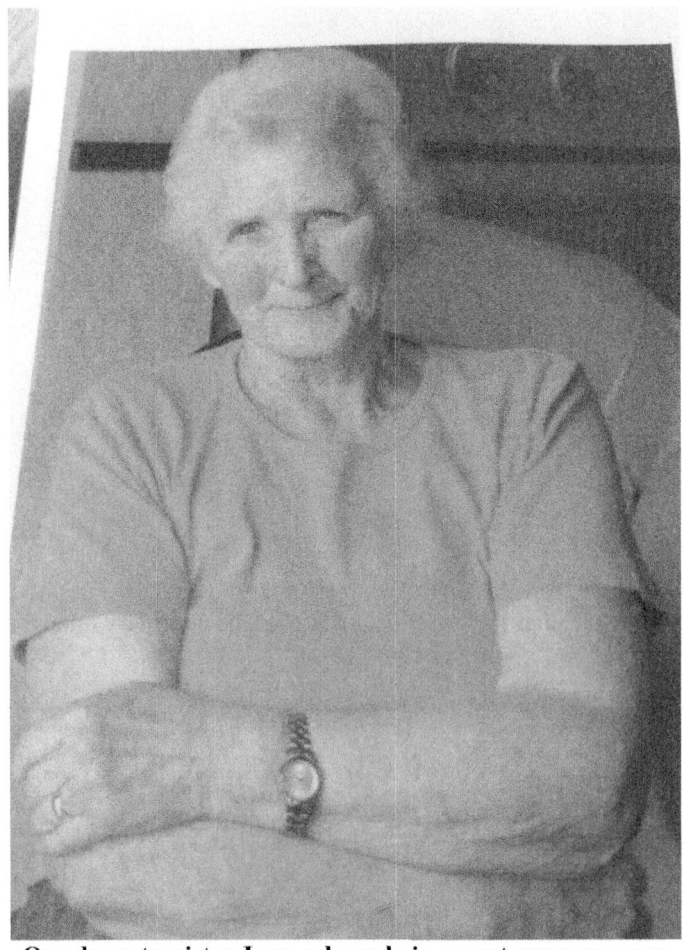

Our dear stepsister Joan, who only in recent years we were able to have contact. A beautiful lady who we have remained in contact with and has been visited by Robert and more recently Brian, who loved her very much xx.

Our eldest brother Robert with his daughter Emma Hazzard and I (Emma and I share the same birthday.)

Brian with Pat, Dennis, Dave and our children, Julie and Gary. "Uncle Brian" loved our children very much and ALWAYS wanted to know how they were and what they were doing.

Friend and fellow musician from Bourne, Lincolnshire, Eddie Lunn, who shared charity gigs with Brian and a "deeelish" guitar!!

Looking up to fellow bass player Rune Moe.

Jamming and giving advice to guitarists. (Young Phil Kelly, now guitarist in his own right in America.)

Musical friends Les Robertson (drummer and "French chef") and Ian Geast (Cliff Richard tribute act, sound engineer and "Reiki master").

Two Brian's together! Brian Bowman from the North-East Shadows Club, Gateshead, UK

Good friends and supporters (among many others) of Brian at the occasion of Pat's funeral reception where Brian not only organised her special service but played music also. (Left to right: Barry Husband, Maureen Husband, Guinevere Daish, Dave, Kevin Harris, Brenda Harris, Linda Andrews, Dave Andrews)

Brian and Justin Daish, talented lead guitarist of the Shadowers and a musician in his own right, who gives pleasure to entertaining many groups of people.

Brian's good friend Jim Walters, a great support to Brian and friends at various concerts, and Jim and his wife Marion (recently passed). Brian was extremely fond of them both.

Picnic and day trip out exploring North Wales, courtesy of Brian's very dear friend and fellow Witness, John Barrows

Brian's good friend and very talented fellow musician Steve Reynolds, member of the Wannabe Shadows group. Steve was admired by many Shadows fans all over the world but tragically passed in his early years, but his music lives on. (Just look at YouTube to experience his tremendous talent!)

Brian with David Harrison, on the occasion of my 60th birthday celebration, where they both participated in music for my special party.
David showed Brian and us his collection of Brian's pictures, with a view of including them in a possible book about Brian's life, but due to many circumstances it was not to be, so David very kindly gave me the album as my birthday present to use as I wish... SO HERE WE ARE!!!!

Thank you, David, for all your wonderful efforts and I am eternally grateful for all your pictures and writings and thank you Carol for giving me permission to use them.

Many thanks to all who attended Brian's funeral, either by being at the crematorium (numbers strictly limited due to Covid-19!) or via webcam link, and for the many words, thoughts and condolences given to us. It is very much appreciated, and we are extremely moved by everyone's love and support XX.

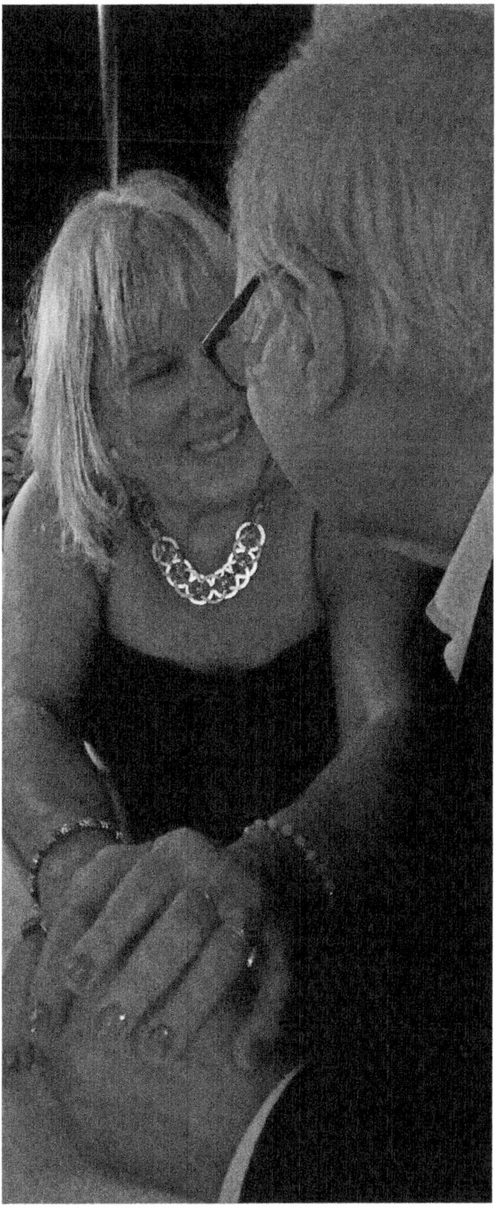

WE SHALL MEET AGAIN.

Printed in Great Britain
by Amazon